Management Extra

CHANGE MANAGEMENT

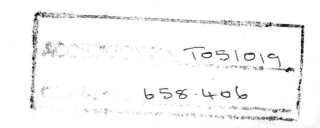

Management Extra

CHANGE
MANAGEMENT

ELSEVIER

eLEARN

Pergamon
Flexible
Learning

AMSTERDAM • BOSTON • HEIDELBERG • LONDON • NEW YORK • OXFORD • PARIS •
SAN DIEGO • SAN FRANCISCO • SINGAPORE • SYDNEY • TOKYO

Elsevier Butterworth-Heinemann
Linacre House, Jordan Hill, Oxford OX2 8DP
30 Corporate Drive, Burlington, MA 01803

First published 2005

British Library Cataloguing in Publication Data
A catalogue record for this book is available from the British Library

Library of Congress Cataloguing in Publication Data
A catalogue record for this book is available from the Library of Congress

ISBN 0 7506 6680 3

For information on all Elsevier Butterworth-Heinemann publications
visit our website at www.books.elsevier.com

Printed and bound in Italy

Contents

Activities

Figures

Tables

Series preface

'I hear I forget
I see I remember
I do I understand'

Galileo

Management Extra is designed to help you put ideas into practice. Each book in the series is full of thought-provoking ideas, examples and theories to help you understand the key management concepts of our time. There are also activities to help you see how the concepts work in practice.

The text and activities are organised into bite-sized themes or topics. You may want to review a theme at a time, concentrate on gaining understanding through the text or focus on the activities whilst dipping into the text for reference.

The activities are varied. Some are work-based, asking you to consider changing, developing and extending your current practice. Others ask you to reflect on new ideas, check your understanding or assess the application of concepts in different contexts. The activities will give you a valuable opportunity to practise various techniques in a safe environment.

And, finally, exploring and sharing your ideas with others can be very valuable in making the most of this resource.

More information on using this book as part of a course or programme of learning is available on the Management Extra website.

www.managementextra.co.uk

A changing world

The world is constantly changing around us, both in our private and our working lives. To manage these changes we develop coping strategies. In your private life you may set aside time for reflection or recreation each week to take stock of where you are. Organisations develop both formal and informal structures, which provide customary ways of reacting to external events. It is these established patterns of behaviour that provide us with a framework and a measure of security in a changing world.

Radical or transformational change

Every so often these established ways of doing things become inadequate and we must make major changes in order to establish a new framework for our lives. In your personal life this may be, say, starting a family or approaching retirement. Organisations may be forced into making radical changes for a variety of reasons, ranging from new competitors entering their markets to advances in the technology underlying their products.

It is these transformational or step changes, which form the subject of this book. The management skills you require for these periods of upheaval differ from those required for day-to-day line management, and it is these skills that we will explore and develop throughout the book.

We will be looking at change management from the perspective both of the organisation and of the individual manager. A central need is for you to make the link between the two, to both stand back and take in the broader perspective and reflect upon your own role in the change management process.

For a business to move from where it is to a new position requires a team effort, and the approach taken in this book is, of necessity, multidisciplinary. It is by building teams drawn from different functions within the organisation that most initiatives are implemented. Because of this, the study of change management provides an opportunity to integrate many management topics, such as the role of learning within the organisation, the need to develop good communication, team building and effective human resource management. In particular, the skills of the operations manager and the project manager are required in the implementation of change.

Your objectives are to:

♦ Understand why change is necessary and your role in the change process

♦ Investigate external and internal forces for change

♦ Explore how to develop and implement a change strategy, including launch strategies, management styles and targeting change

♦ Use your knowledge of individual reactions to change to help you adapt your behaviour and achieve successful change

♦ Adapt your approaches to cultural change

♦ Explore the dynamics of organisational change and how they can be harnessed for success.

1 Why change?

This theme is about change and why we need to change. It is about how change affects organisations; how they can respond to changes in the environment; what questions to ask in an atmosphere of change; and the links to continuous improvement. The search is on for a process we can use to make change smoother and at the same time to gain competitive advantage.

The effects of change upon you as an employee or manager, and how you can contribute to decisions about the organisation's response, all play a full role in the successful implementation of change management.

This theme looks in some detail at the skills and competencies needed to manage periods of transformational change. Your current responsibilities may require some of these change management skills and at some stage in your career it is likely that you will have to act as a change manager. We will explore how change management differs from the operational management of an organisation – not to define some hero-like change manager, but to look at the key management characteristics required in changing organisations.

In this theme you will:

♦ **Explore how your organisation's current culture and practices are the product of its past (perhaps in many ways of its quite recent past)**

♦ **Research trends within your industry**

♦ **Assess the key competencies for change management and contrast these competencies with those required at other times**

♦ **Explain what is meant by continuous improvement.**

Forces for change

At some time in your personal or business life you may have become dissatisfied with the way things were going, or perhaps some external event may have caused you to take a radical change of direction. In these situations you need to spend time thinking about what is unsatisfactory about where you are now, where you would like to get to and how you are going to get there.

For organisations, change management refers to these periods of upheaval when radical action is required if the organisation is to survive and prosper. As with any form of change, it is about moving from where we are now to some desired future state.

It is particularly about:

♦ the purpose of our organisation and our vision of where we want to get to

♦ how we are going to organise ourselves in the future

♦ the means by which we are going to get to this desired future state.

This sounds very grand, but from the perspective of the individual employee, change may appear much less attractive. The employee may feel threatened as their role in the organisation and accepted work practices are challenged. They may feel helpless because despite brave words about participation from management, they feel that change is something that happens to them rather than something in which they participate. Worst of all, the current change may be the latest in a series of initiatives, which can lead to cynicism about management fads.

The challenge for any organisation is to resolve these conflicts and mobilise its workforce to achieve its strategic vision. In an increasingly volatile world, it is this ability to manage change that can separate industry leaders from the also-rans. From a personal perspective, you may need to become as skilled in managing change as you are in managing ongoing operations.

Sources of change

Those of us who have worked for any length of time are aware that the rate of change is increasing. The sort of seismic change experienced by IBM is currently (2001) being experienced by the major telecommunication companies, but compressed into a much shorter timescale. The case of IBM outlined in Table 1.1 shows how organisations must change over time in response to radical changes in their environment.

Period	Company objectives	Management priorities
Early to mid-1980s	Grow and maintain market dominance in the mainframe and mini computer markets	♦ invest in the IBM brand ♦ increase service levels ♦ launch regular new products
Late 1980s to early 1990s	Survive the threat from competitors as personal computers come to dominate	♦ major cutbacks in cost-base ♦ divest peripheral parts of organisation
Mid-1990s onwards	Restart growth	♦ acquire new companies ♦ diversify into software and computer services

Table 1.1 *How IBM's objectives and strategies shifted over time*

Source: *Adapted from Lynch (2000)*

These external or environmental forces for change are one side of the equation. On the other side is organisational bureaucracy and complacency. In static or slow-moving environments, there is a tendency for organisations to become bureaucratic, lethargic and introspective. The need to confront this organisational complacency can be one of the major triggers for change. See Figure 1.1.

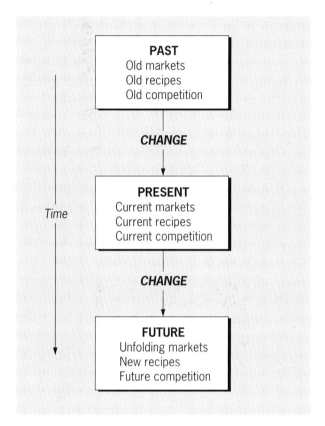

Note: Recipes refers to the established ways in which an organisation anticipates and responds to change. Companies often base change strategies on what has happened in the past three to five years. While it is important to draw lessons from recent history, the author [Grundy] draws attention here to the need to base change strategies on what is going to happen in the future and to develop new recipes or ways of responding to change.

Figure 1.1 *Changing recipes*   Source: *Grundy* (1995)

This rapidly changing environment means that you will have to live through many more periods of major upheaval at work than your predecessors. You need to consider how you will respond to this changing environment, and what it will mean to you. You need to develop new skills to contribute effectively as your organisation goes through periods of turmoil. Finally, you may want to have a say in where your organisation is going, not just about how it is going to get there.

Banking Components Ltd's core business was the manufacture of electronic components, primarily for banks and other related financial services companies. In the 1990s it was the subject of a takeover by Secure Modules Group (SMG), an emerging technology company, and renamed Secure Components Ltd. SMG planned to redevelop Secure Components into a manufacturer of more specialised electronic components and diversify its target markets into the telecommunications industry. Over the following years, the company did supply both

3

the banking and telecommunications markets but continued to operate much as it had done before the acquisition.

Despite significant growth in the telecommunications market, internal performance measures showed inefficiency in business operations. For instance, there were high component reject rates across all lines and agreed delivery dates were not being met. Customers were becoming increasingly dissatisfied with the level of service offered but this was tolerated by the company during a time of high customer demand and low market supply capacity.

Neil has recently joined the company from a competitor. As he has experience of change management programmes, senior management is thinking of asking him to lead a change management programme.

Ask yourself:

♦ *How long can the company expect to meet demand with deteriorating performance?*

♦ *How long will the customer tolerate poor delivery performance?*

Activity 1
A historical perspective

Objectives

This activity will help you to:

♦ explore how your organisation's current culture and practices are the product of its past (perhaps in many ways of its quite recent past)

♦ understand how current culture and practices will not remain in place indefinitely but will need to change (perhaps radically) in the future (and perhaps the not too distant future).

Task

1 Produce a table like Table 1.1, *How IBM's objectives and strategies shifted over time,* to chart change in your organisation. Going back over the last 10 or 15 years, identify the main periods of change, what the organisation's objectives were during the period and the priorities of management. If you are new to the organisation, you may need to find out something of its history. You could do this in an informal way by talking to colleagues who have been with the organisation for some time.

2 What are the current objectives of your organisation? What are the
   main priorities of management in achieving these objectives? Add
   these to the table.

Period	Organisational objectives	Management priorities
Current		

Feedback

Decide whether the changes you have identified occurred
because of:

◆ **external factors**, such as a slump in the market or increased
   competition

◆ **proactive action taken by management**, for example the
   acquisition of other companies or the launch of new
   products.

The priorities may have changed over time from cost-cutting to
increasing sales, to establishing new distribution channels – in
fact, in any number of ways.

Finally, consider the current organisational objectives and
management priorities. Do these include initiatives to change
your organisation? If so, what are the reasons given for making
these changes? You may like to discuss your ideas with
colleagues.

All change

There has always been the need to manage change and it is easy to overestimate the extent to which the scale and rate of change at this point in history is greater than that in the past. The change from an agricultural to an industrial society in Britain, the New Deal initiative to take America out of recession in the 1930s and the need for reconstruction throughout Europe after the Second World War were all times of turmoil that required creative management through the transition period.

However, from the 1960s onwards it is true to say that the periods of stability, when business operations could just be managed, have become shorter, and the necessity to make changes more frequent. The fundamental reason for this is competitive pressure: if an organisation and its products have no competitors, then it is under no pressure to change. This increased competitive pressure has come from such sources as:

- ◆ technological change, both in manufacturing processes and the possibility of new products
- ◆ globalisation, of products, markets and competitors
- ◆ cheaper communication and distribution, particularly the revolution in telecommunications and information technology
- ◆ government deregulation, including privatisation and legislation to promote competition.

Another major source of change, of which you may have personal experience, is the massive increase in mergers and acquisitions activity. Managers, on average, currently face the prospect of going through the process of merging with another organisation two or three times during their working lives.

What does all this mean for you as an individual employee? It means that you are likely to be faced with more frequent periods of transformational change during your career. While we all need to respond to changing circumstances every day, transformational change refers to those periods when an organisation must make radical alterations in the way it does business in order to survive and grow. This book is mainly concerned with these periods of rapid, step changes.

Change management as a discipline

It was the poor success rates in many, if not most, change management programmes that led to the search for a successful recipe for managing change. Management consultants have developed numerous, different prescriptive processes detailing such wonders as the *Ten steps to successfully changing your organisation*. These consultants argue that by adopting what they regard as proven methodologies, organisations can greatly increase the likelihood of success.

Many express great scepticism about these recipes – you may yourself have been involved in such an externally led programme at some stage. Their shortcomings stem from their failure to be context-specific – there is no one way to manage change and every change situation will demand its own unique solution. Change management writer Paul Strebel (1997) makes the point strongly when he says, 'those who pretend that the same kind of change medicine can be applied no matter what the context are either naïve or charlatans.'

Those directly involved in change management maintain that success comes as much from knowing what questions to ask as knowing what has worked in the past. To quote Paul Strebel (1997) again, 'change may be constant but it is not always the same. Different types of change require different responses.'

You may have experience of a major change initiative that has run into the sand or been quietly abandoned after a couple of years. The reasons why many, if not most, change management programmes fail to achieve their objectives is not down to some failure to follow a proven recipe. Instead the most common failures in change management derive from a number of common causes.

Firstly, there may have been insufficient preparatory work carried out on planning the change. Everything from agreeing the need for change and the objectives, to the transition process should be set out and agreed as far as possible before the change programme commences.

Having emphasised the importance of planning, the second common failure is in viewing the process as purely mechanistic, with individuals following the master plan. In fact, employee reactions to change cannot be tightly controlled and the need to take account of organisational culture and to motivate individuals is central to the change process.

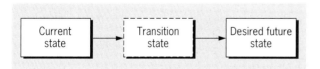

Figure 1.2 *The process of change management*

Finally, there is often a failure to manage the transition state itself (see Figure 1.2). The period when the certainties of current practices are being destroyed and before a new framework is put in place requires a style of management that is very different from the management of day-to-day operations.

This has led to increasing emphasis upon the importance of change management skills. To be a successful change manager you need to:

♦ analyse the need for change both in the external environment and within the organisation

♦ obtain agreement on what is to change

♦ manage the transitional state between current practice and the desired future state.

Towards continuous improvement

It has been argued that the pressure to change is now so frequent that it is necessary to develop processes and cultures where constant change and improvement can take place throughout the organisation.

Change management is a term used when there is an attempt to move faster than the current culture or expertise allows. It should be one of the aims of any change management programme to make the organisation more receptive to future change. In an ideal world this would make future change programmes redundant as the organisation would be attuned to making continuous improvements.

What this means in practice is that you and your fellow managers will need to acquire the necessary skills to both manage operations and periods of change. If the managers in your organisation acquire these skills, then this can become a key competence within the organisation, giving it an important competitive advantage.

Within your own areas of responsibility you may already be feeling the pressure for you to become a change manager in addition to your line responsibilities. You may feel it is no longer sufficient to manage within an established framework, that it is not just desirable but a necessity that your organisation obtains input from all its managers about how it can respond to a rapidly changing environment.

Secure Components' traditional banking market was flat but telecommunications demand was mushrooming.

Efforts to meet demand were frustrated by deteriorating performance measures and deteriorating customer service quality. There had been a series of improvement initiatives in recent years, from quality programmes to business re-engineering. These initiatives had changed precisely nothing but had created a culture of general resistance to change programmes.

In order to break this cycle of failure, senior management asked Neil, an operations manager who had experienced change management programmes in other organisations, for his proposals. Neil recalled that shortly after joining the company, one of the senior managers told him with pride in his voice that 'Yes, they tried TQM here a couple of years back but of course it didn't last long. It was just another management fad. It was all-important until the first missed order, then it was back to business as usual.'

Neil was asked to develop proposals for a change programme to radically improve operational performance and realign the company culture with the faster-moving, less traditional telecommunications market. While pleased to be given the go-ahead, he knew that driving through the necessary changes was not going to be easy.

Ask yourself:

◆ *What conclusions could Neil draw from the senior manager's comment and previous change initiative failures?*

◆ *Between performance improvement and culture change, what was likely to be Neil's biggest challenge?*

The activity that follows focuses on the direction your organisation is taking.

Activity 2
Future change

Objectives

Use this activity to:

◆ research trends within your industry

◆ set down possible futures.

Task

1 Read internal newsletters, the reports in the annual accounts, press reports and any other sources you have to hand to research what your industry may look like in five years' time.

2 In the table that follows, first fill in the current objectives and priorities of your organisation – you can transfer the information you prepared for Activity 1. Next, fill in what you think the organisation's objectives and management priorities will be in five years' time – and speculate, if you can, about what might happen after that.

Period	Organisational objectives	Management priorities
Current		
In five years		
Beyond five years		

Feedback

Managers need to anticipate change and think creatively. We need to create a vision of the future and actively pursue it. The only alternative is to be like a small boat tossed around on the sea as we repeatedly react to the latest external event.

Hopefully, doing this activity has helped you to do some reading and creative thinking about where your organisation is going and how management priorities will change in the future. Other people within your organisation may have different ideas, but that is fine because it is through debate that better-quality decisions will emerge.

The change manager

Books on human resource management often contain a discussion of the different ways of defining what we mean by management and what managers do. For our purposes we will keep it simple and take the key functions of a manager to be those shown in Table 1.2.

Establishing overall purpose and policy	For senior managers this will be the strategy of the organisation, but more junior managers still set the framework for the operations for which they hold responsibility
Organising work, allocating duties and responsibilities	Both for the day-to-day operations and in response to changes in demand, availability of staff, machine/distribution problems etc.
Giving instructions or orders	To this would now be added such terms as team building and motivation of staff
Controlling	Checking that performance is according to plan and taking remedial action where necessary
Co-ordinating the work of others	Ensuring that the work of individuals within the department and the work of the department as a whole integrates with the objectives of the organisation

Table 1.2 *The key functions of a manager*

Look at Table 1.2 and consider whether it broadly describes your work, or perhaps your line manager's work. While the emphasis between the various functions will differ, they probably encompass most of what you do as a manager. The operational manager's sense of their own position and the way they are rewarded reflect these functions.

Managing in stable conditions

Often you and your fellow managers will be judged against budget or other performance measures that emphasise the achievement of measurable performance targets. These may be anything from reaching a certain volume of sales to putting all designated staff through a particular training programme to update their skills.

Certainly it is part of your responsibility to keep abreast of changes in market conditions or technology. You will need to respond to changes in short-term trading conditions or sudden production problems. Equally important, you, together with your line manager, will need to fine-tune the operation of the department under your control in response to long-term changes in the business environment.

Essentially, however, a large part of your job is probably to reduce uncertainty by developing procedures and processes to cover as many eventualities as possible and enable delegation to take place. It is the efficiency and effectiveness of these procedures and processes by which you will be judged.

Managing in times of change

Consider again the basic purpose of change management. Here the aim is to move from our current state to the desired future state. See Figure 1.3.

Figure 1.3 *The process of change management*

To be an effective change manager you need to have the ability to see the big picture without having your judgement clouded by your own position within the organisation. Often organisations will supplement change management teams with someone 'out of the box' – perhaps an external consultant or someone brought in from another company within the group.

As a change manager you need to be able to:

♦ dispassionately analyse the shortcomings of how the organisation currently operates

♦ produce proposals for the direction the organisation should take and the means by which it is to get there

♦ gain acceptance from senior management and, ultimately, the workforce for your proposals.

Nobody is suggesting you can do this on your own. For the moment you are most likely to be asked to contribute to the work of a change management team and you will exercise these skills as you contribute to the work of the team.

The core competencies for managing change identified by Carnall (1999) are outlined in Figure 1.4 and expanded in Table 1.3.

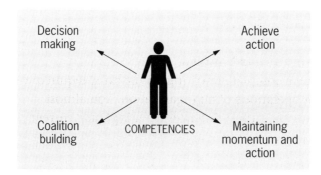

Figure 1.4 *Competencies for managing change at a glance*

Decision making:	Achieving action:
◆ shape a feasible and focused programme of work	◆ handling opposition
◆ make 'imaginative leaps'	◆ motivating people to try new ideas
◆ listen to but resist the doubts of others	◆ providing support for risk taking and experimentation
◆ understand the practical and political consequences	◆ building self-esteem.
◆ synthesise the opinion of different, sometimes opposing, people, bringing out the common ground	*Maintaining momentum and effort: team building*
◆ empathise with the viewpoint of others.	◆ obtaining commitment and generating feelings of ownership
Coalition building:	◆ sharing information and problems
◆ clearing ideas with others	◆ managing the early results to build credibility
◆ gaining supporters	◆ providing feedback on success
◆ bargaining and establishing networks of support	◆ flexibility of style, problem-solving approach
◆ presenting and selling ideas.	◆ trust in the people to solve their own problems
	◆ energising, not directing!

Table 1.3 *Competencies for managing change*   Source: *Carnall* (1999)

Table 1.3 is a formidable list but it represents the competencies required if you are going to make it happen. The skills centre on creativity, negotiating, team building and empowering others. In a major change programme they are all essential elements, but you can start thinking now about the relevance of each competency to your current responsibility and any projects in which you are involved.

Comparing the two styles

The change competencies set out in Table 1.3 represent an extension, rather than a complete rewriting, of the skills required to manage the ongoing operations of an organisation. You almost certainly work in an organisation that is undergoing some current change as it adapts to a constantly changing environment.

There are, however, several key differences in the skills you require as a change manager from those in your more operational role:

◆ risk

◆ culture and power

◆ planning versus evolution

◆ timescales.

We will look at each one in turn.

Risk

In order to achieve the transition, you need to invite people to take risks. Unfortunately, people are generally risk-averse. The fact that the need for a change management programme has been identified means that the necessary development cannot take place in safe, small, discrete steps. Although the framework of the transition phase will have been carefully planned, people are still being invited to take a step into the unknown.

Culture and power

It was Machiavelli who pointed out centuries ago that those who currently have position or power will always oppose change. In addition, those who stand to gain in position and power in the new organisation will be in favour of change, but not as vehemently as it will be opposed by those who stand to lose.

You will need to be attuned to the culture of your organisation. You need to recognise what in the culture gives the organisation strength and what holds it back. You need to become adept at handling the politics of the transformation process.

Planning versus evolution

Partly because of the people issues of the transition, it will not be possible to plan the transition in any neat or tidy way. Where it is essential to involve the workforce in the change process, the next step in implementation may evolve according to the result of the preceding step. Indeed, it is common for the objectives to be amended during the change process as people contribute and buy in to the change.

In addition, where, for instance, new technology or new ways of working with suppliers are being tried, it may be necessary for your team to proceed to some extent by trial and error, learning from each stage as progress is made.

As a change manager you will need to be comfortable with this state of flux, encouraging people to play at trying out possible new solutions. To put this another way, you will not start with a map of the route the organisation must follow but rather take regular compass readings to check that everyone is moving in the right direction. Any attempt to exercise detailed control over the transition process may result in it grinding to a halt.

Timescales

Finally, if you are an operational manager, you may feel that meeting delivery deadlines and other time targets is one of the essential criteria by which you are judged. But focusing too much on meeting deadlines can be counterproductive in change management situations, encouraging participants to seek the familiar in delivering outputs to deadlines.

Certainly key milestones for the transition and an overall timetable for the change will need to be established. Within this framework the workforce and management should be encouraged to experiment and be creative, exploring new ways to do things better.

The change manager as leader

As with any major project, it will be necessary to put someone in overall charge of the change management programme. Some of the writers on change management have emphasised the leadership qualities needed as an essential component of successful change management. Table 1.4 looks at some differences between managers and leaders.

Manager	Leader
◆ is a copy	◆ is an original
◆ administers	◆ innovates
◆ maintains	◆ develops
◆ focuses on systems and structure	◆ focuses on people
◆ relies on control	◆ inspires trust
◆ has short-range view	◆ has long-range perspective
◆ asks how and when	◆ asks what and why
◆ has his/her eye on the bottom line	◆ has his/her eye on the horizon
◆ accepts the status quo	◆ challenges the status quo
◆ is the classic good soldier	◆ is his/her own person
◆ does the right thing.	◆ does the right thing.

Table 1.4 *Managers and leaders: spot the difference*   Source: *Eglin* (2001)

However, the hero figure described under the Leader heading in Table 1.4 is not the only way of managing change. Indeed, given a distinct shortage of heroes in the average organisation, the usefulness of producing such lists is open to question.

More realistic alternatives for appointing someone to head up a change management programme are to:

- ◆ appoint a senior manager from within the organisation; even if an alternative is chosen, it will be essential for the change management programme to be championed by one or more senior managers within the organisation

- ◆ draw on internal change managers; large organisations may have units designed to support periods of rapid change,

15

particularly where the organisation makes frequent acquisitions

♦ bring in external change managers; this has the advantage of bringing in an outside view but in some cases external change managers can be over-prescriptive in their approaches, attempting to use what they have found successful in the past but which may be inappropriate in the current circumstances

♦ put one of the functional heads in charge, whether from HR, quality or operations; such approaches have been successfully used, but the backing of powerful figures within the organisation will be even more important and the functional heads will need to build alliances with managers from other functions.

The work involved in either leading or contributing to change management teams often provides important stages in the development of future senior managers. If you can show comfort with situations of great uncertainty, be willing to take risks and show creativity, then you are displaying many of the most important qualities required in senior managers.

In a study of 130 executives in 55 different companies worldwide, researchers Gregersen, Morrison and Black found that 85 per cent thought change management was a critical leadership capability.

Source: *Black* (2001)

Diversification into the telecommunications market had created unprecedented growth in demand for Secure Components, the specialised electronic components manufacturer.

Meeting weekly demand was an ongoing challenge and was testing the resourcefulness of the company. Operations had expanded several times to keep up with demand, and deterioration in key performance measures seemed inevitable. New equipment had been procured and temporary labour recruited. Factory space was at a premium and expansion plans were being aggressively pursued.

The electronic components manufactured by the company were relatively young in their life cycle and high reject rates had been tolerated by the industry – though no individual company would reveal its own rejection rates.

The company placed great emphasis on inspection to ensure quality. Every week 2.5 million units were either inspected by hand or inspected by specially developed robots. Anxious to meet volume demands, management energy had been focused on the 'realignment of quality standards' – in layman's language, lowering specifications in order to reduce rejection rates.

This action was intended to simultaneously reduce the ongoing reject rates, increase output/productivity and reduce the number of planned 'remake' orders. Yet despite management's efforts, the key internal performance measures continued to show an alarming downward trend.

Initially Neil's task was to improve operational performance. However, it soon became apparent to Neil that the deterioration in operational performance was only a symptom of a much more serious problem.

Ask yourself:

◆ *Was the realignment of quality standards likely to be an acceptable long-term solution to the customer?*

◆ *Was the realignment of quality standards a* leader *or a* manager *response?*

Activity 3
Change competencies

Objectives

Use this activity to look at change competencies and relate them to your own experience. It will help you to:

◆ assess the key competencies for change management

◆ contrast these competencies with those required at other times.

Task

The following table sets out Carnall's (1999) list of core competencies for change managers.

1 In the blank space alongside each section, list instances where you have used these competencies.

2 Consider which of these competencies it would be useful to develop to improve your performance in your current role.

3 Evaluate which competencies would need the most development if your organisation were to ask you to lead a change management project.

Competencies for managing change
Decision making – the ability to: *Your experience:*

◆ shape a feasible and focused programme
   of work

◆ make 'imaginative leaps'

◆ listen to but resist the doubts of others

◆ understand the practical and
   political consequences

◆ synthesise the opinion of different,
   sometimes opposing people, bringing
   out the common ground

◆ empathise with the viewpoint of others

Coalition building – the ability to: *Your experience:*

◆ clear ideas with others

◆ gain supporters

◆ bargain and establish networks of support

◆ present and sell ideas

Achieving action – the ability to: *Your experience:*

◆ handle opposition

◆ motivate people to try new ideas

◆ provide support for risk taking and
   experimentation

◆ build self-esteem

| *Maintaining momentum and effort –* | *Your experience:* |
| *the ability to:* | |

- build teams

- obtain commitment and generate feeling of ownership

- share information and problems

- manage the early results to build credibility

- provide feedback on success

- have a flexible style and a problem-solving approach

- trust in people to solve their own problems

- energise, not direct!

Feedback

If you could list only a few items from your own experience, you are probably underselling yourself. Think of instances where you have had to sell your ideas about getting something changed, times when you have told someone how much you appreciated their help or when you have acted to build up the morale of a team.

In terms of your career development, the ability to handle uncertainty, to negotiate and to empower others are all requirements of senior managers as well as those managing change programmes.

◆ Recap

This theme looks at the reasons why an organisation needs to be responsive to change.

Explore how your organisation's current culture and practices are the product of its past (perhaps in many ways of its quite recent past)

◆ Change is the replacing of a state of affairs that exists now with something different. This change happens over time and the future will not look like the past.

◆ Change management involves the conscious attempt to control, or at least to influence, the change that is going to happen to your organisation.

Research trends within your industry

◆ Successful change management requires you to think about who your competitors will be in the future, what your products will be and how the organisation will organise to meet new challenges.

Assess the key competencies for change management and contrast these competencies with those required at other times

◆ To work as a change manager requires a set of skills or competencies that enables the manager to be effective during a period of flux and during the normal running of the organisation.

Explain what is meant by continuous improvement

◆ The pressure to change is now so frequent that it is necessary to develop processes and cultures where constant change and improvement can take place throughout the organisation.

◆ The organisation and its managers need to have frameworks for continuous improvement in place that allow the organisation to respond rapidly to change.

 **More @**

Campbell, D., Stonehouse, G. and Houston, B. (2002) 2nd edition, *Business Strategy: an Introduction*, Elsevier Butterworth-Heinemann
This is an accessible textbook that provides a straightforward and comprehensive guide to complex issues and concepts. Of particular relevance to this theme is Part 1 'An introduction to the strategic process'.

Dixon, R. (2003) 3rd edition, *The Management Task*, Elsevier Butterworth-Heinemann
This book considers the nature of management and the environment in which management operates. The requirements for effective, successful management techniques are explored, covering many areas – from the need for planning and forecasting, leadership, motivation and communication to control and decision making. See Part 2 'The Management Process' and Part 4 'The Managerial Environment' in particular.

Lynch, R. (2002) 2nd edition, *Corporate Strategy*, Financial Times Prentice Hall
This text explores the dynamics of competitive advantage and the 'dot.com' bubble, customer-driven strategy, resource-based strategy, the development of mission and objectives, and new approaches to knowledge innovation and learning.

Business.com – www.business.com/directory/management/ change_management/reference/
This is a business-focused search engine and directory. There are a number of articles and references on change management which may be of interest on this site including: 'Why do employees resist change?' and 'Creating temporary organisations for lasting change'.

Management first – www.managementfirst.com/ change_management/index.htm
Management first is a resource primarily for subscribers to Emerald journals. However, there are a number of articles available free of charge on the site. Try out the section on change management.

Full references are provided at the end of the book.

2 The conditions for change

Before change can take place, there must be people within the organisation who recognise the need to change. This may be because of some concrete event such as a collapse in sales or it may be no more than a general feeling of unease despite reasonably good current performance. This theme begins by looking generally at types of change and external, internal and proactive triggers for change. The next sections focus more closely on the external and internal environments for change.

> Increasingly, a winning strategy will require information about events and conditions outside the institution. Only with this information can a business prepare for new changes and challenges arising from sudden shifts in the world economy and in the nature and content of knowledge itself.
>
> **(Drucker (1997) quoted in**
>
> **Paton and McCalman (2000)**

You will explore the strategic and external environment and the link between strategic planning, change management and environmental analysis.

You will also discover some of the theories associated with diagnosing change situations and the characteristics of each stage of the evolutionary cycle of competitive behaviour.

Having completed the environmental analysis you need to carry out an analysis of the internal operations of the organisation. As with the environmental analysis, the aim is to inform the change management programme and put it firmly into the framework of your organisation's strategy.

In this theme you will:

◆ Distinguish between different types of change and identify suitable responses

◆ Prepare an analysis of the current and future environment of the industry in which your organisation operates

◆ Evaluate what needs to change if your organisation is to compete in this new environment.

The impetus for change

Organisations experience change every day as, for instance, orders are taken from new customers, employees join or leave and production schedules are arranged. The subject of this theme is the type of change that cannot be handled within the normal procedures of the organisation.

In this type of change, due to external or internal pressures, the organisation must make fundamental changes in the way it does business. It may be necessary to throw away the rule book during these periods of transformational change. There will be disagreement not only about what needs to be done but also about what is happening and even about what the organisation should be trying to achieve.

For instance, Ralph Stacey (1996) distinguishes between three different types of events:

Closed change, where there is certainty about what happened, why it happened and what needs to be done.

Contained change, where we are reasonably confident about what happened, why it happened and what needs to be done about it.

Open-ended change, where there is wide disagreement about what happened, why it happened and what is to be done about it.

Closed change

When we look back at the history of an organisation, there are some sequences of events that we can clearly recount in a manner commanding the widespread agreement of the members involved. We are able to say what happened, why it happened, and what the consequences were. We are also able to explain in a widely accepted way how such a sequence of events and actions will continue to affect the future course of the business. We will call this a closed change situation.

Such closed change would normally apply to the continuing operation of an existing business.

For example, consider a business that supplies pop CDs and tapes to the teenage market. Managers in that business are able to say with some precision how the number of customers in that market has changed over the past and furthermore how it will change for the next fifteen years or so. Those customers already exist. The managers can establish fairly clear-cut relationships between the number of customers and the number of CDs and tapes they have bought and will buy.

Contained change

Other sequences of events and actions flowing from the past are less clear-cut. Here we find that we are able to say only what probably happened, why it probably happened and what its probable consequences were. The impact of such a sequence of events upon the future course of the business has similarly to be qualified by probability statements.

For example, the supplier of CDs and tapes will find it harder to explain why particular kinds of CDs and tapes sold better than others. That supplier will find it somewhat difficult to forecast what kinds of tapes and CDs will sell better in the future, but market research, lifestyle studies and statistical projections will enable reasonably helpful forecasts for at least the short term.

Open-ended change

There are other sequences of events and actions arising from the past and continuing to impact on the future where explanations do not command anything like widespread acceptance by those involved.

The company supplying CDs and tapes may have decided in the past to diversify into video film distribution by acquiring another company already in that business. That acquisition may then become unprofitable and the managers involved could well subscribe to conflicting explanations of why this is so.

Some may claim that the market for video films is too competitive. Others that the diversification was a wrong move because it meant operating in a different market with which they were not familiar. Others may say that it is due to a temporary decline in demand and that the market will pick up in the future. Yet others may ascribe it to poor management of the acquisition or to a failure to integrate it properly into the business or to a clash of cultures between the two businesses.

What that team of managers does next to deal with low profitability obviously depends upon the explanation of past failure they subscribe to.

Source: *Adapted from Stacey* (1996) *quoted by Senior* (1997)

Triggers for change

If it ain't broke, don't fix it.

This is good advice in a stable situation. The problem in a constantly changing world is that what worked satisfactorily last year may be completely inappropriate in new trading conditions. Alternatively, while a process may not be 'broke', our competitors may be doing it much better, a situation the organisation cannot live with indefinitely.

If you work in a relatively stable environment, the future may be reasonably predictable, which means that your organisation can plan in the traditional way. Many organisations go through periods of stability. More usually, however, your organisation will be subject to frequent changes in its business environment that act as external triggers for change. Your senior management can also anticipate these external pressures by undertaking programmes that act as internal triggers for change. Finally, there are proactive triggers for change, where an organisation attempts to go out and change the environment in which it operates. Each of these triggers for change is considered in the sections that follow.

External triggers for change

Changes in the business environment are the most obvious triggers for change. The boom in the telecommunications industry during the 1990s led to the development of a management style in the industry geared towards continuous year-on-year growth. The subsequent reversal of fortunes in early 2001 left many of the companies floundering as to how to adapt in an environment requiring retrenchment and, often, refinancing.

Managers within your organisation need to continually scan the environment for changes in the economic environment, the technology, the political situation and social culture. Most important of all is to monitor the competition – if you are not getting better faster than the competition, then your organisation is moving backwards.

Benchmarking is a technique for comparing processes with those in other organisations. For instance, you might compare how much it costs to process a single sales order or the efficiency of IT arrangements. The temptation is to compare with competitors, but this is not always best:

- the information may be commercially sensitive and your competitors may not release it (or may positively seek to mislead you)
- your competitors may be better than you, but other organisations in related industries may be very much better still.

So, the aim is to compare your own organisation with the best in class for the particular function you are investigating. Useful benchmarking can often be done more informally and fairly quickly using the 80/20 rule. Discussions with sales staff who attend conferences, articles in the technical press and feedback from customers can all provide useful information.

Internal triggers for change

Businesses are not just helpless vessels attempting to cope with the stormy waters in which they operate. They can decide to make internal changes so as to compete better. Examples of internal changes might include:

- a new marketing strategy, perhaps trying new methods of communicating with customers
- the introduction of new advanced manufacturing processes
- establishing a different organisational structure.

All these internal changes involve changing the formal organisation and the informal 'this is the way we do things around here' organisation.

Proactive change

Change is not always a reaction to external or internal events. The organisation may be performing well but seek to perform even better. This may be because the organisation wants to act in anticipation of changes which it can see coming down the road in the next few years. Alternatively, it may be that the organisation wishes to go out and actively alter its business environment to its own advantage.

This is proactive change, where the organisation sets out to influence and manage its environment. Examples of proactive change might be:

- Lobbying the government on proposed legislation or to have current legislation amended. Companies active in the field of pollution control devices do not just wait for new government legislation, they will lobby the government, providing their technical expertise to influence the shape of the final legislation.

- Attempting to influence public opinion on health or lifestyle matters so as to project a positive image of the organisation. This can be dangerous ground, but the major oil companies, for instance, are reluctant to let environmental pressure groups make all the running.

- Increasing the global spread of operations or branching out into different products are examples of companies attempting to counteract the effect of an economic turndown in one region or product by diversifying.

- Developing new technologies which change the ground on which companies compete. For instance, Hewlett Packard (HP) actively pursues disruptive innovations, which will create new markets. The role of its research arm 'is not only to create advances to support HP's current applications, but to create "disruptive" technologies that establish entirely new businesses' – for HP its 'people personify the word invention'.

Source: *Wolf* (2001)

Finally, in proactive change the senior management may go out to manufacture a trigger for change with the intention of shaking staff out of their perceived complacency. Thus, the organisation may divest certain operations, radically restructure the organisation or introduce new reward systems.

The deterioration in operational performance was a symptom of Secure Components' inability to adapt to meet the new demands placed upon it. It was therefore necessary to develop a change programme proposal that targeted the root cause of the problem, and not the symptoms.

Neil knew that he had to overcome the negative feelings and attitudes generated by previous change programme failures and the grass roots resistance to further change programmes. 'We're too busy to get involved in any more change programmes. Can't you just let us get on with the job!'

During this period of rapid growth in the telecommunications market, customers were tolerant of poor delivery and Secure Components was making record profits. There appeared to be little justification, or enthusiasm, for a change programme.

Having developed an understanding of the marketplace and of how Secure Components operated, Neil concluded that the company would be at risk if there were a future downturn in the telecommunications market. Significant efficiency and productivity improvements would be required to reduce the impact of any downturn.

Neil recognised the need for change and, importantly, recognised the need to create a symbolic change that would avoid the resistance to 'yet another change programme' – a symbolic change which would communicate the message, 'we are serious about change and this time change is actually going to happen'.

But how was Neil to develop his change strategy and, most important, convince the board of directors that his proposals were suitable, acceptable and feasible?

Ask yourself:

◆ *'If it isn't broken, don't fix it.' When is this bad advice?*

◆ *What types of triggers for change are at play in Secure Components?*

Activity 4
Types of change

Objectives

This activity asks you to:

♦ distinguish between different types of change

♦ identify suitable responses.

Task

1 From your own experience, think of three events that you know of within your organisation that fall under each of the three headings in the table below.

2 Consider how the organisation responded to this type of change, and note your observations in the second column.

Type of event	How the organisation responded
Closed change	
1st event	
2nd event	
3rd event	
Contained change	
1st event	
2nd event	
3rd event	
Open-ended change	
1st event	
2nd event	
3rd event	

Feedback

When faced with an important problem that directly affects you, it is all too easy to think that you know the right answer. If only people could understand what you were trying to get across.

In the worst situations, people may concentrate on building their own army to support a particular analysis and proposal for action rather than going out and talking to people.

This activity should have emphasised that it is only the routine, day-to-day decisions that have definite answers. As soon you begin to look at the wider challenges facing your organisation, then everything becomes much more subjective and the scope for disagreement that much greater.

Environmental triggers for change

Here we will look more closely at how you can analyse your organisation's current position and the forces for change in its environment.

Strategic context

In 1999, Johnson and Scholes described strategic planning as a three-stage process. See Figure 2.1.

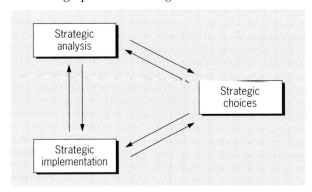

Figure 2.1 *The three stages of strategic planning*

Source: *Adapted from Johnson and Scholes* (1999)

Thus strategic planning involves three different steps or activities:

◆ carrying out an analysis of the environment and of the resources at the organisation's disposal

◆ developing different strategic choices and evaluating their attractiveness for the organisation

◆ implementing the preferred strategic choice.

The arrows point both ways in Figure 2.1 because the three steps are not intended to denote a sequence of activities. Thus in developing strategic choices, your organisation may need to go back and do further investigations of its environment. Difficulties in implementation may cause your organisation to rethink its objectives or develop further possible strategic choices.

When you propose a change management programme, senior management will look closely to ensure that it integrates with the overall strategy of the organisation. Your change programme must be part of the implementation of the organisation's strategies and be undertaken to achieve its objectives. In addition, a successful change management programme may create further opportunities for an organisation, enabling it to generate additional strategic choices and even rethink its objectives.

For example, a company underperforming in a niche market may come to dominate that niche after a change management programme which, for instance, makes it more customer focused. This new-found competence may cause the company to decide to compete outside of its traditional niche, perhaps acquiring another underperforming company in a related area to which it can apply its new-found competence in change management.

Environmental changes

You can use much of the strategic management toolkit to analyse an organisation's environment to provide a firm basis for action. Figure 2.2 shows an organisation's business environment.

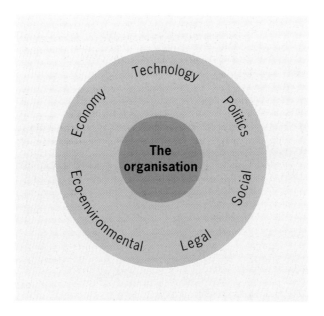

Figure 2.2 *The business environment*

For instance, a PESTLE analysis can be used to identify external triggers for change. As trading conditions become more volatile and change more rapid, so organisations need to continually scan their environment for the political, economic, social and technological

changes that will impact particularly upon their business. The
factors for change in a PESTLE analysis are shown in Table 2.1.

Changes in the economic environment	There will be short-term, cyclical changes demanding fast reactions such as cost cutting or firefighting to meet sudden surges in demand
	But there are also the long-term structural changes in the economy, such as:
	◆ underlying growth and inflation rates
	◆ globalisation of markets
	◆ regional economies such as the EC and the euro
	◆ de-industrialisation
Technological changes	The huge reductions in information costs produce both opportunities and increased pressures
	Technological advances reduce the entry costs into many businesses
	Shorter product life cycles with increased scope for new products and methods of distribution make more opportunities available to all organisations in an industry
Political changes	The trend in numerous countries towards moving public enterprises into the private sector is a major source of change. But under this heading one could also include:
	◆ deregulation of markets
	◆ moves to introduce private sector practices into public organisations, such as the UK Government's Next Steps initiative
	◆ regional conflicts
Social changes	Broad changes in the way we live, including:
	◆ greater emphasis on health and safety
	◆ environmental concern
	◆ social equality
	◆ demographic changes
	◆ change away from the nuclear family
	◆ values and lifestyle choices
Legal/legislative changes	Changes in the legislative framework within which the organisation operates, including:
	◆ health and safety and other employee legislation
	◆ product liability legislation
	◆ legislation directly affecting an organisation's market, e.g. regulations on telecommunications
	Increasingly in the UK, the legislation may be putting EU directives into effect, i.e. implementing changes agreed at a supranational level
Eco-environmental	Concern for the environment now constitutes a major element of the framework within which organisations operate. Influences upon particular organisations may include:
	◆ the opportunity to develop new markets and products, e.g. the supply of pollution-control equipment for motor cars and other applications is now a major industry
	◆ designing products so that they are environmentally friendly
	◆ the increasing cost of meeting pollution and other environmental regulations

Table 2.1 *PESTLE analysis: possible factors for change*

Carefully consider how the factors in the PESTLE analysis affect your
organisation. Try not to view them as some static background
against which the business operates but as an environment which is
constantly developing and moving.

For instance, e-commerce and the Internet would have appeared on
few environmental analyses in the early 1990s but the technology

had been developed and its use was growing at that time. In the late 1990s, its impact would have appeared under the heading technology for almost all organisations. In 2001, with the bursting of the dot.com bubble, it would still probably appear, but as a longer-term, less pressing force for business change.

One of the drawbacks of PESTLE analysis is that it can become too focused on the historical or current environment. When using such tools as PESTLE analysis, Porter's 5 forces or SWOT, always try to model the current environment and then redraw the model for what you think the business environment will look like in three to five years. The change management triggers are then those changes needed to transform your organisation to be able to compete in those future models.

Diagnosing change situations

Strebel (1997) sets out an industry model of an evolutionary cycle of competitive behaviour (Figure 2.3) where companies within the industry compete at different times on product innovation and cost efficiency.

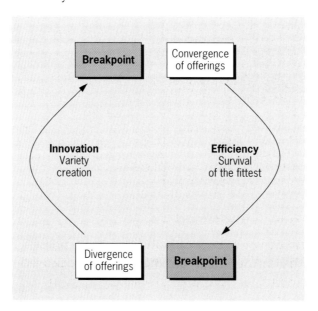

Figure 2.3 *Evolutionary cycle of competitive behaviour*

Source: *Strebel* (1997)

Each stage in the cycle has its own characteristics. These are set out in Figure 2.4.

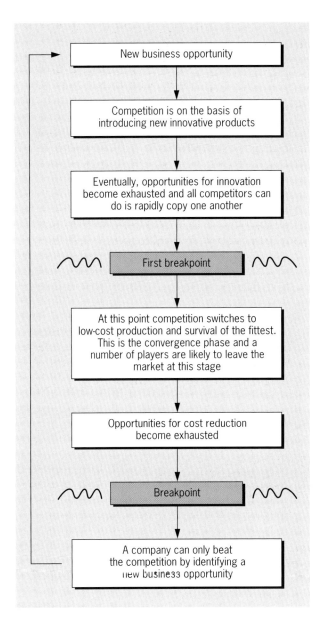

Figure 2.4 *Characteristics of the evolutionary cycle*

Thus the cycle of competitive behaviour involves two main phases. One is divergence or the innovation phase when someone discovers a new business opportunity. The second is the convergent phase where companies compete on price.

Strebel (1997) gives the example of the personal computer industry where technological innovation can lead to the rapid introduction of new products followed by price cutting and an attempt to become the lowest-cost producer.

You will find the analysis particularly useful to predict changes in the market to which your organisation must respond. Set out in Table 2.2 are some suggested early warning signs that change may be imminent.

Convergence	Divergence
Competitors: increasingly similar products, services and image	Customers: a saturated market is accompanied by declining growth rates and restless customers
Customers: the differentiation of offerings appears increasingly artificial and market segmentation starts breaking down	New entrants: restless customers are attracting new entrants
Distributors: bargaining strength shifts downstream to the distributors	Competitors: declining profits may cause them to try innovative offerings or withdraw
Suppliers: cannot provide a source of competitive advantage as everyone knows their inputs	Suppliers: new resources and, especially, new technology are frequently the source of a divergent breakpoint
	Distributors: lag behind because they need to adapt to the new offering

Table 2.2 *Leading indicators for divergence or convergence*

Source: *Adapted from Strebel by Senior* (1997)

Divergence is more difficult as it is based on a new offering that does not yet exist. To spot these new offerings before they are introduced, you may need to read the trade press, talk to others in your industry and think creatively about how what you offer your customers may change in the next few years.

From scanning the marketplace and observing how the company operated, Neil had seen that Secure Components would be very sensitive to a downturn in the marketplace. He believed a proactive change programme could significantly reduce the business risk of a downturn and enhance the company's competitive position in the marketplace.

A detailed environmental analysis revealed that the technology in which the company specialised was in the convergent phase. Rigorously defined industry standards had severely limited product innovation opportunities. As demand currently outstripped supply, there was in any event little incentive to innovate.

Currently, competitor differentiation was largely based upon the ability to supply. There was evidence of new suppliers entering the market and that the mobile phone market was becoming saturated. The government had recently auctioned the third generation (3G) mobile communications licences for very considerable sums of money and the financial stability of major telecommunications companies was being questioned.

Neil concluded that a market downturn would have significant implications for any company that was not prepared. Companies in the future would need to be operationally efficient, flexible and responsive to a changing environment.

To complete his strategic analysis and develop realistic strategic options for the company, Neil needed to assess the strengths and weaknesses of the company. He needed to perform an internal analysis of the company's resources and core competencies.

Ask yourself:

◆ *What was the nature of the environmental risk facing Strategic Components?*

◆ *What further external information might be useful to the design of a change management programme?*

Activity 5
Analysing the environment

Objectives

Use this activity to:

◆ prepare an analysis of the current environment of the industry in which your organisation operates

◆ prepare an analysis of what you think the environment will look like in five years

◆ list what needs to change if your organisation is to compete in this new environment.

Task

1 Use the first column of the chart that follows to produce a PESTLE analysis for your own business based on your industry's current environment. Try to make this as specific to your organisation as possible. For example, if the revolution in information technology is affecting your business, think about the areas in which it has most impact – is it, for example, in the delivery of the service to customers, reducing your cost base or developing new products?

2 Having completed your analysis, in the second column set out what you think the main environmental factors will be in five years' time. Think about how they will influence what you sell and the way you produce or provide it. Think about how demand might be affected and how your suppliers may change.

3 Finally, think about the changes your organisation needs to make to compete in this new environment. Will your industry even exist in five years?

PESTLE analysis	Current environment	Future environment
Changes in the economic environment		
Technological changes		
Political changes		
Social changes		
Legal/legislative changes		
Eco-environmental changes		
The prospects for your business – how far it will need to change:		

Feedback

Organisations which appear to epitomise good practice and security one year can fall from grace with amazing speed. Think of Marks & Spencer, Marconi or Cisco, the Internet systems provider.

As organisations work away on improving the fundamentals of their business, they need to be aware that those fundamentals may be undergoing rapid change and the nature of the business itself transformed. For example, as the introduction of personal computers decimated the market for mainframe computers, so commentators now regularly speculate about what will replace the PC.

You could use your work on this activity as a basis for discussion with colleagues in your organisation. What do your colleagues think? How far is there agreement as to what major environmental change may impact upon your business over the next five years?

Internal analysis

A change management consultant brought in from outside the organisation would obviously need to find out about the internal functioning of the organisation before preparing their recommendations. As an insider, who has perhaps worked for the organisation for some time, there may be a temptation for you to skip this step.

Scope of internal analysis

There is a danger here that your knowledge is limited or coloured by your functional background or particular career path. Everyone has their own prejudices and you may bring your own to the task. As a result, you may be selective in your choice of data and from whom you seek information.

Whether internal or external staff carry out the work, there is a clear need for a systematic approach to the task. At the same time, the aim is not to document current processes in detail for the following reasons:

- ◆ Such an approach would be costly, time-consuming and may duplicate existing documentation that is adequate for the purpose.
- ◆ You are carrying out the investigation because there is a perceived need to change current practice. If this is the case, why document it?

The amount of detail and the scope of the investigation will be governed by the nature of the area identified as a possible candidate for a change management programme. For instance, if an organisation's distribution systems is under investigation, it will probably not be necessary to look in detail at purchasing or production processes. However, if the organisation is trying, for example, in some way to move to being more customer focused, then this will probably require changes in all parts of the organisation.

In order to see the wood for the trees, it is useful to consider the key factors for success in the industry in which your organisation operates. Use Table 2.3 to help you.

Low-cost operations
Are we low-cost operators? How do we compare with competitors? Aldi (Germany) and Somerfield (UK) are both low-cost supermarket operators
Economies of scale
Do these exist in the industry and how important are they? For example, large-scale petroleum chemical refinery operations such as those operated by Royal Dutch/Shell
Labour costs
Does our industry rely heavily on low labour costs for competitive operations? For example, Philips (Netherlands), which has moved its production to Singapore and Malaysia
Production output levels
Does our industry need full utilisation of plant capacity? For example, European paper and packaging companies
Quality operations
Do customers need consistent and reliable quality? McDonald's has applied the same standards around the world in its restaurants
Innovative ability
Does our industry place a high reliance on our ability to produce a constant stream of new innovations? For example, computer hardware and software companies such as Apple, Epson and Microsoft
Labour/management relations
Is our industry heavily reliant on good relations? Are there real problems if disputes arise? For example, European large-scale steel production, at companies such as Usinor
Technologies and copyright
Does the industry rely on specialist technologies, especially those that are patented and provide a real competitive advantage? For example, News Corporation (Australia) which has exclusive global control over the decoder cards for satellite television and as a result has a virtual monopoly in some countries of viewer payment satellite channels
Skills
Does the organisation possess exceptional human skills and people? For example, advertising agencies and leading accounting companies

Table 2.3 *Identifying key factors for success*

Source: *Adapted from Lynch* (2000)

You will need to determine which of the key performance indicators in Table 2.3 are relevant for your organisation and direct your fact finding accordingly. It is achieving excellence in delivering these key factors that will enable the organisation to beat the competition at the end of the change programme.

Resource audit

Before you start, establish the scope of what you are being asked to investigate – is it a fairly narrow operational matter relating to your own department or do the issues cut across several departments? The areas to be investigated and the amount of detail you go into will be driven by the need to produce your recommendations. Do not spend time investigating areas that lie outside your terms of reference, that is, what you have been asked to do. If you think the scope is too narrow to address the underlying problems, then ask that the scope be widened.

The areas for investigation are shown in Figure 2.5 and will cover some or all of the issues in Table 2.4.

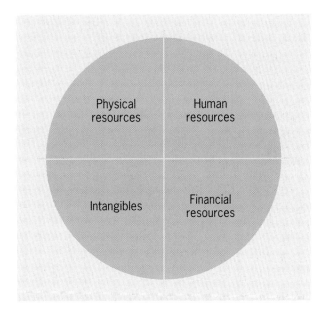

Figure 2.5 *An organisation's resources*

Physical resources	◆ What is the age and condition of our plant or equipment?
	◆ How does possession of this plant give us competitive advantage?
Human resources	◆ What skills do we have, and how many people have them?
	◆ How adaptable and innovative is our workforce?
Financial resources	◆ What are our relationships with our shareholders, banks and other providers of finance?
	◆ Financial strength can be a source of competitive advantage, allowing an organisation to pursue strategies not open to its competitors
Intangibles	◆ What goodwill does the organisation possess?
	◆ This may be the organisation's greatest asset, particularly in a service organisation

Table 2.4 *Resource issues*   Source: *Adapted from Johnson and Scholes* (1999)

The information you gather about these different resources will be useful for recommending both:

- ◆ what the objectives of the organisation should be in this area
- ◆ how to achieve those objectives, for example, the skills possessed by the workforce and their adaptability are key considerations when planning the change process necessary to achieve the recommended objectives.

Drawing conclusions

We have warned about the dangers of analysis paralysis. Your analysis must be tailored according to the purpose for which it is being carried out and the context in which it is made.

For change management programmes, the following three factors are particularly important considerations in drawing together the conclusions:

Core competencies and resources

What are the core resources or competencies of your organisation which give it competitive advantage? What resources do you want to retain and strengthen as part of the change management process? Are there resources which were crucial in the past but which you think might now be redundant?

Capability for change

What is your organisation's capability to undergo change? Have the managers/workforce shown themselves to be adaptable in the past? For instance, to what extent do promotions take place from within the organisation?

Resources for change

What resources do you think will be made available to undertake the change programme? Are all your fellow managers complaining of overfull workloads at the current time? If this is the case (and it usually is) how is time to be freed up to work on the necessary changes?

Barriers to change

Your analysis may lead you to conclude that a particular course of action is definitely worth doing. But while arguments in favour of what you are proposing may seem very strong to you, never underestimate the potential resistance to change.

Try to see your proposals through the eyes of other individuals within your organisation. Who might oppose what you are proposing and why? Who might not openly oppose but seek to obstruct if change is attempted? Who has most to lose from what you are proposing? What political power do they possess to oppose and/or obstruct your recommendations?

Neil needed to perform an internal analysis of the company's resources and core competencies in order to complete his strategic analysis.

He identified that there were primarily two parts to the organisation. The first was research and development (R&D), which provided technology and product leadership in the marketplace; the second was operations, where Neil worked, which produced and marketed the final product.

Whereas R&D was technology and quality led, operations was low cost and quality led. Each had developed its own distinct micro-culture. R&D was about adopting and exploiting change through technology innovation. Operations was about driving down cost through volume and efficiencies. It was clear to Neil that the company's core competency was technology innovation and not operations.

The company's planning procedures assumed low-quality work and high rejection rates. Besides, operatives knew that any defectives would be found and remedied during final inspection. Accountability and responsibility for their work had effectively been abdicated. The typical reject rate was 40 per cent, and occasionally exceeded 80 per cent! When challenged, the operations director declared, 'this is typical in our business'.

Furthermore, operators were grouped into functional areas and avoided communication with operators from upstream or downstream processes. Teamwork capability was virtually non-existent.

Neil concluded that operations was in desperate need of a major makeover, but what strategic option(s) could he develop that would be suitable, acceptable and feasible?

Ask yourself:

♦ *What are the key barriers to change?*

♦ *How would you rate the organisational capability for change?*

Activity 6
Key resources

Objectives

This activity will help you to:

◆ evaluate the key success indicators for your industry

◆ produce a list by category of the key resources.

Task

First, for your industry, rate the nine key factors for success set out below in order of importance, 1 being least important and 9 being very important.

	Importance								
Low-cost operations	1	2	3	4	5	6	7	8	9
Economies of scale	1	2	3	4	5	6	7	8	9
Labour costs	1	2	3	4	5	6	7	8	9
Production output levels	1	2	3	4	5	6	7	8	9
Quality operations	1	2	3	4	5	6	7	8	9
Innovative ability	1	2	3	4	5	6	7	8	9
Labour/management relations	1	2	3	4	5	6	7	8	9
Technologies and copyright	1	2	3	4	5	6	7	8	9
Skills	1	2	3	4	5	6	7	8	9

In the light of this ordering, summarise those resources in your organisation which give you strength in the important key factors for the industry as a whole. Think also about where you are weak.

	Strong	Weak
Physical resources		

	Strong	Weak
Human resources		
Financial resources		
Intangibles		

Finally, what does your organisation need to change to be the top organisation in your industry?

Changes needed:

Feedback

What is important here is not how comprehensive the analysis you have carried out, but whether you have identified the key factors that can differentiate you from the competition.

All organisations in your industry will need a certain level of resources to compete at all. Depending on the industry in which you operate, you will need, for example, skilled personnel, plant and the ability to develop new products.

But what do you do better than the competition? Or, where does the potential lie within your organisation to do things better?

Finally, remember you will want to develop key resources for the way your industry will look in the future, not to fight yesterday's battles.

◆ Recap

This theme examines the types of change and the factors in the external and internal environment that trigger change in organisations.

Distinguish between different types of change and identify suitable responses

- Different types of change call for different responses. It is therefore important to identify what it is you are dealing with when you analyse a situation

- Three different types of change are identified: closed, contained and open-ended change.

Prepare an analysis of the current and future environment of the industry in which your organisation operates

- All long-term planning requires organisations to find out about their environment. In change management we are concerned not only with the current situation but also with how the world will look in the future.

- A PESTLE analysis can be used to analyse external triggers for change.

- The evolutionary cycle of competitive behaviour can be used to identify and predict changes in the market to which your organisation must respond.

Evaluate what needs to change if your organisation is to compete in this new environment

- For the purposes of a change management programme, you need to focus on the key success indicators for your industry and then evaluate the resources at your disposal.

- The final stage is to predict any barriers to change and develop strategies to overcome them.

▶▶ More @

Campbell, D., Stonehouse, G. and Houston, B. (2002) 2nd edition, *Business Strategy: an Introduction*, Elsevier Butterworth-Heinemann
This is an accessible textbook that provides a straightforward and comprehensive guide to complex issues and concepts. See Chapters 4 and 5 for products and markets, including market segmentation, product life cycles and new product development. See Chapter 6 for a new view on SWOT and PESTLE analysis – SPENT analysis.

Johnson, G. and Scholes, K. (1999) 5th edition, *Exploring Corporate Strategy*, **Prentice Hall Europe**

This is a classic work on corporate strategy. You may find it useful for future reference. Throughout the text, strategy is seen through three complementary 'lenses': 'design' (an analytical approach); 'experience' (builds on cultural, institutional and cognitive schools of thought); 'ideas' (builds on evolutionary and complexity theories).

Paton, R. and McCalman, J. (2000) 2nd edition, *Change Management: a Guide to Effective Implementation,* **Sage Publications**

The second edition of this textbook for change management uses current examples and a more strategic focus to guide students through the issues and processes associated with managing change.

Porter, M. E. (1980) *Competitive Strategy: Techniques for Analysing Industries and Competitors*, **The Free Press**

Porter shows how competitive advantage can be defined in terms of relative cost and relative prices, thus linking it directly to profitability, and presents a whole new perspective on how profit is created and divided.

Williamson, D., Jenkins, W., Cooke, P. and Moreton, K. M. (2004) *Strategic Management and Business Analysis*, **Elsevier Butterworth-Heinemann**

This text provides a road map for the strategic analysis of a company or organisation. It identifies the key strategic questions and provides clear guidance on how they may be answered. See Part 1 'The Four Big Questions You Need to Ask', and Part 2 'Helping You Answer the Four Big Questions' for an analysis of organisation structure, strategic processes and competitive advantage.

The Change Management Resource Library – **www.change-management.org/articles.htm**

This website offers a wide range of useful and interesting articles on the subject of change management. For instance:

◆ 'ADKAR' – change management model for consultants, project leaders and managers; excellent overview of this new change management approach.

◆ 'Do you need a complacency check-up?' by Dennis Hoppe How complacency, settling for mediocrity, and stagnation can severely damage your company.

◆ 'The Changing Workplace: How Flexible is Your Company?' by Ellen M. Riccardi The working world is changing fast. New technologies and realigned work environments are altering the way companies do business and the relationships between workers and their employers.

Full references are provided at the end of the book.

3 A framework for change

This theme is about the process for change, presenting recommendations and gaining approval for change. As we shall see, this is more than a preliminary step to the real action of implementation. How the programme is sold and agreed at this stage may have profound implications for the success of the project as a whole. You will need to understand how strategic choices are made and proposals are evaluated within your organisation.

Once you have gained approval for the chosen change management programme, your next task is to plan in greater detail for the transition from the organisation's current state to the desired future state. You will explore the content of this change strategy and the work that surrounds its preparation.

The framework of change management used throughout this theme is that of moving from the current state through a transition process to a future state.

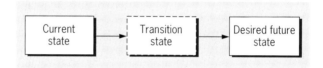

This theme investigates further how organisations make the movement from the current to the future state. In particular, we will look at the 'Three Step Model' developed by Lewin (1952) based on unfreezing the organisation, moving and sustaining the change.

In this theme you will:

♦ Generate possible alternative strategies for change and formulate recommendations as to which is the best alternative

♦ Describe the importance of the way in which approval is gained to later stages of the programme implementation

♦ Develop ways of involving others and gaining their commitment to change

♦ Evaluate how to deliver each of Lewin's three stages of change in the context of your own organisation.

Getting the go-ahead

Here we look at presenting your recommendations for a specific change programme and gaining senior management's approval.

Strategic choice

The recommendations you, or your task force, make to senior management will present them with an option which they can then accept or reject, or ask you to revise.

There are always a number of options open to an organisation at any point in time. Different companies in the same industry may pursue different market strategies, technologies and human resource approaches. Some strategic choices will provide the foundation for lasting competitive advantages, others may bring the company to its knees.

Therefore, there is no one right way to implement the organisation's strategy for achieving its goals and vision. It is the responsibility of senior management to choose between alternatives, each of which will have their advantages and disadvantages. Your recommendations may have been carefully researched but because the decision concerns the future, it will always be made on the basis of incomplete information and must take into account the risks associated with failure as well as the benefits of success.

Implementing a change management programme, particularly if it is an organisation-wide programme or it brings in fundamental changes, is a strategic choice. Senior management must decide whether this is the best strategic choice or whether an alternative, including the option to do nothing, offers a better return/risk prospect.

Evaluating proposals

In order to evaluate the attractiveness of a major change proposal, Johnson and Scholes (1999) identify three areas, which centre on the following questions:

- *Suitability* – does it address the circumstances in which the company is operating?
- *Acceptability* – does it offer a good return on the investment needed, does it carry an acceptable level of risk and will stakeholders in the business react favourably?
- *Feasibility* – can we actually do it? Do we have the necessary resources and capabilities?

47

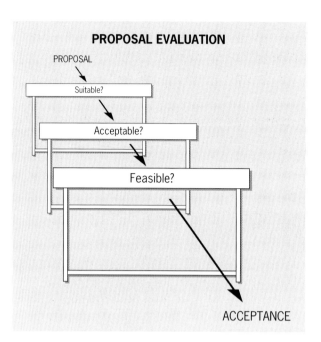

Figure 3.1 *Evaluation hurdles*

Look at the case study about Asda – the UK grocery retailer.

Asda's Open Plan

In fast-moving businesses, a 'command and control' approach to strategy selection may be too inflexible. There may be a need to focus selection of strategies much more at the business unit (or departmental) level.

In 1991, when Archie Norman became CEO of Asda, he inherited dwindling customers and mounting debts, and the company looked ready to close its doors. However, by 1996 it had become a much more open business with a management team that claimed to listen to both customers and staff. Performance had been transformed – with the company back in the black and a 30 per cent rise in customers.

The new approach was nurtured by de-layering management to shorten the line between stores and head office, and also by changing the way that departments were organised. For example, each in-store department, such as the bakery or fishmongers, had its own profit and loss account. Head office functions were also split into business units (e.g. for meat, drink or clothing), each of which, in turn, was split into smaller categories (e.g. spirits, wines and soft drinks). In each category, the buyers and the head of marketing work with category (product) managers to develop their business.

The overall aim had been to move from the 'command and control' approach by senior management, to what they called an 'inform and involve' culture. This took several forms. There were listening groups on current issues and listening surveys of staff and customer opinion. Instead of the old-style weekly managers' meetings, they had twice-daily 'huddles' between managers and their work teams to plan ahead. There was a 'tell Archie' suggestions scheme which attracted 14,000 ideas in the first 18 months.

The style of senior management combined a high degree of approachability with the readiness to take informed decisions. Colleagues were expected to challenge management decisions and to take decisions of their own. Communication had also been improved in many small ways from newsletters to customer compliments, and an ample number of open and inviting meeting rooms.

The working environment was open, with plenty of opportunity for informal meetings, stimulating creativity and sparking off ideas. It was all part of 'getting rid of the treacle' of the old approach.

Source: *Management Today* (1996)

Taking the example of the change programme undertaken at Asda, the original proposal for 'getting rid of the treacle' might have been assessed as shown in Table 3.1.

Suitability

In 1991 the company needed to attract new customers and reduce its debt mountain. The proposals were suitable in that they sought to offer an improved level of service to customers and establish profit responsibility centres within each store

Acceptability

Archie Norman came to the store with a high reputation in the City and among investors. The new strategy did not involve changing the core business in which the company operated but 'doing it better'. External stakeholder reactions were therefore favourable

Through the open style of management, much thought was obviously given to selling the new way of doing things to the workforce and existing management

Finally, financial projections on the proposal would have been made which would have shown, as happened in practice, acceptable financial returns by the company

Feasibility

But could Asda make the proposals work? Senior management obviously took the decision that the new open style of management could be made to work or they would not have gone ahead. Alternatives such as selling the business would have been held in reserve in case the expected benefits from the change management programme did not materialise

Table 3.1 *Evaluating Asda's proposals*

The exact way in which change management proposals are evaluated will differ according to the scope and nature of the particular proposal. Note in general how, even if the end result will be judged in hard financial terms, at the centre of the change programme is an attempt to change the culture of the organisation.

Gaining approval

Looking at the Asda case again, Archie Norman was a highly regarded business leader and his approval of the change management programme was essential for its ultimate success. However, there is danger in having personality-led changes.

Personality-led change is about accepting the need for change because 'Archie says this is a better way of doing things'. The danger with this approach is that the acceptance of the need for change is shallow because the workforce has not been asked to make an assessment of the situation and 'buy in' to the need for change.

Asda made the transition from personality-led change to situation change. Through an open style of management and the extensive involvement of staff, Asda employees came to agree on the need for change and became willing participants in the change process.

If you are to act as a change agent then you must be prepared to sell the proposal to the key decision makers in the organisation. You must first identify the key decision makers and power holders in the organisation. Then you will need to get your key points across succinctly and forcefully.

It is always a good tactic to emphasise the pain that management and the workforce are feeling with current practices so that the need for change is accepted and the picture of a brighter future looks more attractive. This pain may be anything from poor financial performance, to losing customers, or to the inability to develop and launch new products within acceptable timescales.

Proactive change, where an organisation is not currently feeling serious pain, is much more difficult to sell and will require more extensive consultation and selling of the benefits. Here, incontrovertible external evidence may be a powerful persuading tool. For instance, research into product development by competitors may show that the company is living on borrowed time if it does not have its own developments in the pipeline.

Finally, formal approval from the top is not sufficient, and if obtained in isolation, may prove to be the first nail in the coffin. Senior management will normally want proof from the change manager that you have talked to the key people in all areas that will be affected by the programme. Not all may be enthusiastic at this stage, but you must show that wide consultations have taken place and that there is a reasonable chance of building momentum for the launch of the change programme.

In conclusion, if you are to contribute to selling a possible change management programme, you will need to be skilled in communicating, influencing people and carrying out negotiations. While the benefits may be clear to you or your team, others may need to be persuaded and brought on board. To achieve this, you may also need to develop your listening skills – others will have their own important contributions to make.

> Neil now needed to combine his external and internal analyses as a basis for his recommendations to senior management. The external analysis was used to prepare a powerful argument that some action needed to be taken, and to paint a bleak 'do nothing' option.
>
> By presenting a strategic option, which took account of the published company strategy and management team aspirations, he achieved both strategic fit and political fit. Perhaps his greatest insight was to involve key middle management players throughout the analysis and option development phase. Middle management involvement achieved further political fit and a strong sense of ownership on their part.
>
> Neil's proposal was to tackle the operations issues head on.
>
> Firstly, he reinterpreted the company's key business objectives of 'customer satisfaction', 'profitability' and 'adapting to change' into change programme imperatives of 'focus on the customer', 'we are here to make money' and 'we must learn to work smarter'.
>
> Secondly, he needed operations to learn teamwork and communication skills, and to take responsibility for their own work.
>
> Thirdly, he needed to orchestrate a major change event that would clearly communicate that 'this time change was really going to happen and there would be no going back'.
>
> He concluded that a factory rearrangement into cells, the empowerment of the workforce and the elimination of quality control (QC) were the radical change measures that would be required to address the company's sensitivity to a market downturn.
>
> The formation of operations cells would enable cross-functional teams to form that were focused on the whole operations process. Empowerment of these teams would enable them to take ownership of change in their own environment. Removal of QC would remove the psychological safety net between operations and the customer, and drive responsibility and accountability within these teams.
>
> Benchmarked data from other industries suggested that significant improvements in reject performance, productivity and on-time delivery could be achieved through the introduction of operations cells.
>
> This careful packaging and marketplace context enabled Neil, with the support of middle management, to sell this strategic option unanimously to the board of directors.

Activity 7
Choosing the strategy

Objectives

This activity asks you to:

♦ generate possible alternative strategies

♦ formulate recommendations as to which is the best alternative.

Task

Take an existing proposal for change within your organisation. Alternatively, if you have your own proposal for change that you would like to put forward, use that. Either way, choose a proposal that has wide-ranging implications for your organisation – perhaps a new organisational structure, new product development or a cost-containment exercise.

First, briefly state the objectives and scope of the proposal.

Objectives and scope:

In the table below, set out your appraisal of this proposal against the criteria of suitability, acceptability and feasibility.

Suitability

Acceptability

Feasibility

Feedback

Suitability is all about whether what is proposed furthers the aims of the business. Do you consider the proposal meets this criterion or is it a pet project of someone within the organisation? Does it address yesterday's problems and not the way the market will look in 12 months? Do you consider perhaps that the proposal is primarily about internal organisation and does not relate enough to serving the customer?

To be practical, the proposal must be acceptable to all the stakeholders, not just senior management or those most directly affected. Have you thought through exactly who will be affected by the proposal? Have they been consulted and their agreement obtained? If not, how is the programme to be sold?

Some organisations will refuse to consider any proposal for an IT project unless an individual is named who has the time to lead the implementation. Where resources are scarce, the best ideas are of no use unless they are feasible, that is, there is the possibility of successful completion.

Developing the change strategy

As you read, think yourself into the role of a change manager; you are in charge of a team responsible for a change management programme, which will fundamentally change the way the organisation does business. What do you need to put in place before starting to implement the actual changes?

Fundamental requirements

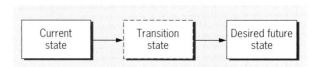

Figure 3.2 *The process of change*

Experience of change management programmes shows that it is the degree of care with which everyone involved prepares for the transition stage of the project that is most likely to separate a successful from an unsuccessful change programme.

> **To fail to prepare is to prepare to fail.**

As the change manager with overall responsibility, you should start the development of the change strategy with a high level of agreement in a number of areas:

- The action area – in a programme to improve relations with key customers, one does not want, for example, production declaring that the programme has nothing to do with them.

- The external and internal analyses, which have been carried out on the action area. It will almost certainly happen at some point that a manager will say to you, 'OK, but I never really agreed with your analysis of that situation – I always thought the real problem was X'. It may happen, but by agreeing the analysis at this stage, disagreements at a later stage can be minimised.

- Outcomes broadly agreed – it is in the nature of change management that the future state to which the organisation wishes to move cannot be spelt out in detail because its exact nature will evolve during the transition. Even though where the organisation is going will be refined, there is still a need to establish a clear idea of the general direction before one starts.

- Management commitment must be obtained – the key players must agree to what is going to be set in motion. Again, there is always a chance that not all will be in favour, and one or two are likely to pay only lip service, but the effort must be made to gain the support of all managers and if this is not forthcoming, it is time to rethink the whole programme.

◆ Timescales – unrealistic or tightly defined timescales can be very demotivating for members of the team, with the implementation reduced to a constant grind of meeting the next deadline with little time to reflect or experiment. At the same time, the world moves on, and some time frame needs to be established if the programme is to be completed before it becomes out of date.

In summary, you will need to balance developing an excellent understanding of how the programme will evolve, without dooming the project to failure by being over-prescriptive and setting the details in concrete.

To be a change manager, you will need to learn how to be a facilitator rather than a director of operations. To do this you will need to develop your influencing, negotiating and listening skills. It will be necessary at times to hide your frustration at what you perceive to be shortcomings in the understanding or performance of colleagues, so that they can develop at their own pace and take ownership of the change process. At other times, you will need to meet people halfway, compromising on what you believe to be right so that everyone can move forward together.

Building blocks

Your plan for achieving the change management objectives is likely to be made up of building blocks and milestones (see Figure 3.3). These building blocks may be initiatives that take place across the whole organisation, for instance, company-wide training programmes. They may also be the responsibility of a specific function, say the implementation of new systems for placing orders with suppliers.

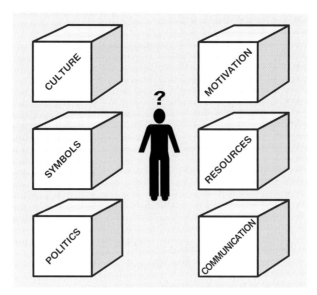

Figure 3.3 *Planning the programme*

Again, some may look like conventional projects, say the commissioning of new plant, while others may be softer, such as setting up cross-functional teams to review employee attitudes to improving communication within the organisation. Some of the building blocks may even be largely symbolic in intent, such as dressing down every Friday.

Changes to the culture of the organisation may be one of the most important aspects of the programme but it is likely to be the most difficult area for you to plan. Often the targets are soft, for instance making people more receptive to new ideas or more customer focused. It will be necessary for you to say what action you propose to trigger changes in the culture but if this is too directed, the action can look like manipulation by senior management.

Resource requirements

A major part of senior management's commitment to the change process is evidenced by their willingness to release resources to the programme. You must obtain a clear commitment that staff seconded to the team will not be withdrawn at the first problem or crisis.

To make this possible, part-time staff may have to be recruited to keep the day-to-day operations of the business functioning. Often the only way is for staff to simply work more hours during the evolution of the new organisation. In this case, it will be even more important that they remain motivated, and feel that their contribution is valued and that there is a pay-off at the end of the process.

New skills are almost certain to be needed as part of the transition but it is not necessary for all the skills to be in place before the transition takes place. Training too far in advance of the actual change can lead to loss of motivation and a lack of retention of what has been learnt.

Recruitment and retention of staff during this period should be focused on the requirements of the new state of the organisation and not on current needs. The skills needed for the future may focus more on acting as a member of a team and being open to situations of flux rather than the more specialist or functional skills of the past.

Gaining commitment

We have already mentioned the importance of releasing resources as a sign of senior management commitment. It is not enough for management to say, 'we agree, go ahead and do it' or even 'we will not stand in your way'.

Particularly where a step-change to current practice is required, you will need to get those with positions of power in the organisation to sign up to the development strategy.

From the moment of agreement you must ensure all decisions taken are consistent with the change programme. You will need constantly to check for divergences and challenge them as soon as they occur. If, say, a key member of the change management team is promoted and leaves the team, then this must be justified and the change manager must be able to explain the situation.

When the change starts to gather momentum it will usually be essential that you involve the whole workforce and that they take ownership of the change process. It is therefore necessary to develop a consistent, effective communications strategy, perhaps using a range of channels such as team meetings, newsletters and e-mail.

What really helps, as with any new venture, is to get off to a good start.

Neil, with the support of his middle management team, had sold the change programme to the board of directors. But this was just the start; Neil and his team now had to work out exactly how it was all going to happen!

Neil had learnt from his past experiences of change management programmes.

He obtained early agreement on the scope of the programme, that is, a decision on what areas would or would not be affected by the change programme. In addition, he invested a lot of time obtaining wide agreement for his strategic analysis in order to limit future resistance to the programme in times of difficulty.

He knew from bitter experience that senior management commitment to a major change programme was imperative.

Commitment would require ongoing and public evidence. Evidence of decision making that supported the programme was necessary together with ongoing support of reasonable requests for special project funding and release of human resources. Neil appreciated that sometimes immediate commercial needs would be contrary to the change programme, but he made it clear that he was looking for 80 per cent support or better. He later learnt to continually scan management activity and was not shy to 'cry foul' when it was needed.

A key concept for which he gained agreement was that as resources (including labour) were saved through change, these would be reinvested into the change initiative to further accelerate the rate of change.

Neil knew that if he was able to create a credible and robust change programme framework, and effectively communicate it to key stakeholder groups, it would engender a confidence that would withstand many of the anticipated setbacks that such a programme would be sure to encounter.

A good start is imperative to all ventures into the unknown, and this would be no exception. Neil needed to ensure a good start and to raise confidence levels that would launch the change programme on to bigger and better things.

Ask yourself:

♦ *How did Neil do his best to ensure that resources would be available throughout the programme?*

♦ *What represents tangible evidence of management support for change initiatives?*

To be continued...

Activity 8
Gaining commitment

Objectives

Use this activity to help you to:

♦ develop ways of involving others in change

♦ develop ways of gaining the commitment of others.

A central part of developing the change strategy is to gain the involvement and commitment of management and the workforce. If change is to evolve during the change process rather than be dictated from above, it is the different groups that go to make up the organisation who must take ownership of, and develop, the change programme.

Case study

Read through the following case study.

Fortunately for Mobil, it had Charles Bennett, a new production foreman at High Island, off the Gulf Coast. A respected engineer, he had worked his way up from his first job with the company as a technician in 1981. Believing that you do not get much out of a production crew by peddling management motherhoods about cost efficiency, empowerment, and shareholder wealth, he talked to his people about the hard work ahead.

'OK guys, we just went through a layoff here and saw our friends go down the road. Do you understand why that happened? We were not competitive, our production costs were out of line.

'Our stake in this is a three-year deal – three years to deliver on our share of the $300 million target. The ball is in our court. Now we can do something about it. We can't make any guarantees that it will save our jobs, but we can sure go down singing.'

On the heels of this sobering message, Bennett also shared information about how management saw the business, and its actual cost position.

'I said: "look guys, I don't want to make accountants out of you, but you've got to understand the business, and how what you do every day affects these indicators. We had lifting costs in '91 at High Island of $1.52 per BOE (barrel of oil equivalent). Guys, we have to do better than that." I was consciously talking business in front of them. What does lifting costs mean? What does cashflow mean? They had never seen any of these kinds of numbers before, or how they affected them.'

By comparing Mobil's costs position with that of its competitors, Bennett showed his crew what could be in it for them. He convinced them that they could become the cheapest operator in the Gulf of Mexico and eventually take business from other companies, which meant more jobs.

'We can beat these guys! And every time we do it, it means more jobs, so let's do it! We can get better here at High Island, we can be the very best in our area. Now, if we do that, guys, that equals jobs.'

This was not an isolated communication. Getting the message across involved Bennett in talking to a lot of people, over and over again.

'They don't get it in one presentation; they get it sitting on the handrail of the drilling platform with you out there drinking coffee with them, and you ask them, "What do you think about this? Does it make sense?" You've got to live it with them every day. It takes a lot of intense focus to influence people.'

Charles Bennett exemplifies one of the most distinctive qualities of the best change leaders: they find a way to turn brutally unpleasant facts into team performance. Ordinary managers may be good at benchmarking analysis or financial projections, but it is only real change leaders who can connect with the minds and hearts of their people, find the simple words that calm anxiety and instil courage, and maintain the trust needed to bring about lasting change.

Source: *Katzenbach* (1996)

Task

Answer the following questions:

1 What techniques did Charles Bennett use to gain the trust and involvement of his team?

2 What were the fears of the individual worker and how did he counter them?

3 Identify some additional areas that Charles might need to address to successfully change the operation.

Feedback

There had been recent redundancies, which must have left the workforce shaken and defensive. Charles did not say 'this is history' but addressed their fears head-on, explaining why the redundancies had taken place. He tried to convey the way the senior managers saw the business in terms of lifting costs and cash flow – he was not talking down to anyone. In positive reinforcement, he explained what it would take to have job security and how it was possible to beat the opposition. Finally, he repeated and repeated his message in different ways; this was not an academic argument, he was trying to win the hearts and minds of the workforce.

Charles was obviously a hands-on manager who 'walked the talk'. It is not enough to be right about what you think needs to be done; you need to persuade everyone involved that what you are proposing addresses their fears and priorities. Even after all this effort, you may still only get a sullen acquiescence from some, but if sufficient numbers of people go with you, then you can build the momentum for change.

This extract is about just one dimension of the change process. To be effective, Charles had to also work with fellow managers on other oil rigs and senior management. Senior management had to both feel that he represented them and be willing to trust him to manage his part of the business.

Making the organisation move

Here we will investigate further how organisations make the movement from the current to the future state. In particular, we will look at the Three Step Model developed by Lewin (1952).

Lewin's model

You may have been involved in action improvement programmes which achieved improved levels of performance in the short term but where practices soon slipped back to their previous pattern. Perhaps the change involved events where new practices were introduced with evangelical fervour and everyone came back resolving to change their ways. After a year or so people had difficulty remembering exactly what the event was all about.

Lewin (1952) noted that this was often the case and argued that a successful change project should involve three steps:

1 Unfreezing the present level.

2 Moving to the new level.

3 Re-freezing that new level.

Even though change is now more frequent than in the 1950s and the idea of re-freezing can be questioned, the model still proves useful for looking at change situations.

To start the process, first try to form a mental picture of what it will be like to work in the future state of the organisation. This vision will then provide both a rationale for why the organisation should change and a means of communicating that need to everyone. In order to communicate the vision, it must be memorable and the use of examples, metaphors or analogies can be useful.

Some of the most famous vision statements include that of Komatsu, the Japanese earth moving equipment manufacturers, who wanted to 'encircle Caterpillar'. Caterpillar was the industry leader in Komatsu's sector at the time. Similarly, Honda wanted to become a second Ford, a pioneer in the automotive industry.

Source: *Balogun and Hailey* (1999)

Jack Welch – without doubt one of the world's most effective business leaders of the last 10 years – articulated his vision of General Electric in the following terms:

'A decade from now I would like General Electric to be perceived as a unique, high-spirited, entrepreneurial enterprise – a company known around the world for its unmatched levels of excellence. I want General Electric to be the most profitable, highly diversified company on the earth, with world-quality leadership in every one of its product lines.'

Source: *Quoted in Sadler* (1995)

Unfreezing

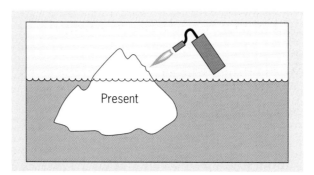

Figure 3.4 *Unfreezing the present*

The notion of unfreezing recognises that before new behaviour can be successfully adopted, the old has to be discarded. Lewin particularly emphasised the importance of the individual who must feel positively the need to change.

Not everyone will want to unfreeze the organisation. The existing culture may not encourage innovation. There may be powerful people within the organisation who perceive they have a lot to lose from any change. At the same time, we do not want to change for the sake of change; we want to keep what is valuable about the current organisation.

It is your job as a change agent to unfreeze the organisation by reinforcing the forces for change and reducing the forces against change. To achieve this you might use a number of levers, some of which are outlined in Table 3.2.

Questioning and challenging the status quo	Possible tools here are: ◆ the use of workshops to broaden discussion and bring out dissatisfactions ◆ benchmarking certain processes or using adverse press reports ◆ 360-degree appraisals where staff appraise their managers
Symbolic breaks with the past	The launch strategy might include a change with a strong symbolic content such as introducing common terms of employment for all staff
Dramatic measures and shock tactics	A radical restructuring of the organisation might be undertaken to show staff they have no option but to change, often with further restructuring taking place as the change management process progresses
Communication, education and training	Internal newsletters about competitive pressures and training programmes in new ideas may all help to break the mould

Table 3.2 *Unfreezing the organisation*

Moving

Having unfrozen the organisation, we must now move it through the transitional state. Managing in this transitional state is very different from managing in stable environments.

Many writers and practitioners argue that you cannot really plan in the conventional sense during this stage but that the process is one where change emerges from the interactions of different individuals and groups. The change manager in this view is seen strictly as a facilitator who intervenes to guide and stimulate the activity of others.

To intervene effectively, the change manager must again use levers and triggers. These are actions by the change manager, small in themselves, which stimulate others to act and take responsibility for those actions. See Figure 3.5.

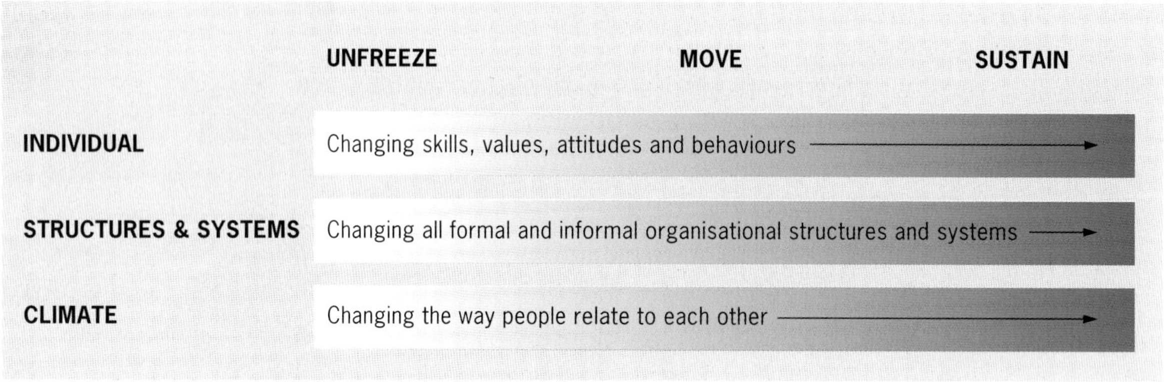

	UNFREEZE	MOVE	SUSTAIN
INDIVIDUAL	Changing skills, values, attitudes and behaviours ⟶		
STRUCTURES & SYSTEMS	Changing all formal and informal organisational structures and systems ⟶		
CLIMATE	Changing the way people relate to each other ⟶		

Figure 3.5 *Designing and sequencing levers and mechanisms*

Source: *Adapted from Goodstein and Burke* (1991)

by Balogun and Hailey (1999)

Here the writers identify the three main areas for action if change is to be achieved and sustained. This is a holistic model of change management; by this we mean that the three different areas all interrelate, with progress in one area held back or facilitated by progress in another. For instance, changes to the formal organisational structure may send important signals about the need to change the culture of the organisation, or an individual may recognise the need for personal change only when the culture around them starts to transform.

There is also a constant tension between the current state we wish to unfreeze and the future state which we wish to maintain. Peter Senge (1992) likens it to an elastic band joining the current and future states. The creative tension of change either results in the vision being brought down closer to the current reality or – the desired outcome – the current reality being raised to the vision.

Re-freezing

The final stage is for management to signal that the change management process has been completed and that it is time to operate within the context of the new culture and processes.

To do this management will need to:

♦ celebrate success and communicate their appreciation of the staff

♦ show by their actions that they will only operate according to the new ways of doing things

♦ support staff in their new roles and reward them accordingly

♦ encourage staff to reflect on the change programme as a basis for further improvements in the future.

Once you have achieved an important task, it is all too easy to just move on to the next problem. If someone has done a good job, then take the time to tell them how much you appreciate their work. At the conclusion of an important project, make the time to hold a party and celebrate success.

Limitations of the model

Lewin's Three Step Model probably works best when change is either proactive or conditions sufficiently stable for the change to take place over a reasonable time period. In more turbulent conditions where external pressures on the organisation's performance or even its survival are more obvious, the model is less useful. Here the unfreezing stage may have to take place by direction from above because of time constraints. Due to lack of time, resources and information, it may be possible to put in place only the broad outlines of the programme with the new state of the organisation emerging from the change processes themselves.

Finally, Balogun and Hailey (1999) consider the model most useful when asking questions, and suggest the following.

Key questions to consider when designing unfreeze, move and sustain:

1 Is there a coherent strategy understood and shared throughout the organisation?

   ♦ Is it in actionable parts and has the sequence been sorted out?

2 Are supporting structures and systems under development?

   ♦ Are new structures to be implemented now or allowed to evolve?

   ♦ What new measurement and reward systems are needed?

3 Is there a trigger for change or has one been manufactured?

   ♦ Has the launch strategy been designed?

4 Are there visible 'early wins' designed into the change process?

   ♦ If so, we must balance attractiveness with implementation difficulty.

5 Are day-to-day activities aligned to get required outputs?

   ♦ Managers may not be aware of all the day-to-day routines.

6 Are the identified barriers to change being removed/dealt with?

   ♦ If so, what are the levers for change and at what stage will they be tackled?

7 Are changes supported with symbolic activity?

   ♦ All stages should have their own symbols.

8 Is communication built into the change process?

   ♦ A variety of communication methods will need to be adopted at each stage.

Neil decided that he needed to refocus people's attention away from the uncertainty of change and onto the future state. He developed a vision of the future that captured the essence of the programme and to which people could relate.

'We will learn to work smarter, to create a lean operation that focuses on exceeding our customers' expectations, and establish ourselves as the best in the business.'

This message was reinforced throughout the preparation, implementation and transition phases of the change programme, establishing it as the standard against which the legitimacy of actions and decisions were judged.

Previous change programmes had failed and Neil decided that the deep-rooted associations between change and failure had to be firmly broken. He would need to develop a launch strategy that provided a powerful and symbolic statement that things were 'going to be different this time'.

He also recognised the importance of maintaining a very high level of communication to continually reassure and reinforce. A series of interactive workshops, briefing sessions, formal presentations, newsletters and frequently updated notice boards were all utilised. Neil argued that traditional levels of communication sent the message that it was 'business as usual', and that relevant and timely communication was the lifeblood of any change programme.

Too much focus on the detailed management of the transition phase was also a potential danger. Helicopter skills were essential; Neil needed to continually scan for changes in the internal and external environment. Changes that acted to support the need for the programme had to be communicated to further justify people's efforts, and changes that undermined the programme needed to be explained in an appropriate context to minimise their adverse impact.

During the programme there was a downturn in the telecommunications market and Neil used this as a powerful reinforcement for the change programme. He also had to deal with enforced commercial decisions to divert all available resources to process a series of strategically important customer orders. Neil was a realist: he understood the realities of balancing the need to improve with commercial realities.

Ask yourself:

- *People will always worry about how change will affect them; how can their thoughts be distracted from the uncertainties of change?*
- *What can be done to reinforce that the company is entering a new phase and that it is not 'business as unusual'?*

Activity 9
Unfreeze, move and sustain

Objectives

Use this activity to:

◆ evaluate the planning of a change programme

◆ recommend possible remedial/further action.

Task

Evaluate a change management programme which is currently taking place within your organisation against the questions below. These are posed by Balogun and Hailey (1999). If no such programme is currently taking place, then ask colleagues about a change management programme completed in the past, or evaluate one of which you have personal experience.

Question	Response
Is there a coherent strategy understood and shared throughout the organisation? ◆ Is it in actionable parts and has the sequence been sorted out?	
Are supporting structures and systems under development? ◆ Are new structures to be implemented now or allowed to evolve? ◆ What new measurement and reward systems are needed?	
Is there a trigger for change or has one been manufactured? ◆ Has the launch strategy been designed?	
Are there visible 'early wins' designed into the change process? ◆ If so, we must balance attractiveness with implementation difficulty.	
Are day-to-day activities aligned to get required outputs? ◆ Managers may not be aware of all the day-to-day routines.	

Question	Response
Are the identified barriers to change being removed/dealt with?	
◆ If so, what are the levers for change and at what stage will they be tackled?	
Are changes supported with symbolic activity?	
◆ All stages should have their own symbol.	
Is communication built into the change process?	
◆ A variety of communication methods will need to be adopted at each stage.	

Source: *Balogun and Hailey* (1999)

Feedback

Where you have identified shortcomings for:

◆ a current programme – what action should be taken to remedy the situation?

◆ a past programme – how far does the shortcoming explain any difficulties encountered?

It is not possible in an activity such as this for you to carry out a full appraisal of a major change programme. Asking these questions and considering the ramifications of negative answers will help you to formulate your own list of criteria for successfully managing change.

◆ Recap

Generate possible alternative strategies for change and formulate recommendations as to which is the best alternative

◆ Some strategic choices will provide the foundation for lasting competitive advantages; others may bring an organisation down. There is no one right way to implement the organisation's strategy for achieving its goals and vision.

◆ Implementing a change management programme involves strategic choices about direction and priorities.

Describe the importance of the way in which approval is gained to later stages of the programme implementation

◆ In order to evaluate the attractiveness of a major change proposal, Johnson and Scholes (1999) identify three areas of concern: suitability, acceptability, feasibility.

◆ A firm foundation for change which includes appropriate backing from key decision makers, external triggers and wide consultation, is essential.

Develop ways of involving others and gaining their commitment to change

◆ As a change manager you need to gain high level agreement to change in a number of areas: the action area, through external and internal analyses, the desired outcomes, management commitment and agreement on timescales.

◆ To be a change manager you will need to learn how to be a facilitator rather than a director of operations. You will need to develop your influencing, negotiating and listening skills.

Evaluate how to deliver each of Lewin's three stages of change in the context of your own organisation

◆ Lewin's model involves three steps: unfreezing, moving and re-freezing.

◆ To achieve change you need to ask whether there is a shared understanding of the change, whether structures are in place to support the change, and whether there are visible early wins.

 **More @**

Balogun, J., Hailey, V. H., Johnson, G. and Scholes, K. (2003) 2nd edition, *Exploring Strategic Change*, Financial Times Prentice Hall
Exploring Strategic Change focuses on the implementation of organisational change and the management of organisational transitions. It seeks to move beyond the formulation of strategy by taking the planning stage through to implementation. The text examines the change process from analysis of context and the diagnosis of needs through the stages of transition and transference to practical change.

Kirkpatrick, D. L. (2001) *Managing Change Effectively*, Elsevier Butterworth-Heinemann
Managing Change Effectively details specific approaches and methods for making change decisions and getting changes accepted. From communication to participation, Kirkpatrick shows managers and executives how to make change their ally.

Paton, R. and McCalman, J. (2000) 2nd edition, *Change Management: a Guide to Effective Implementation*, Sage Publications
The second edition of this textbook for change management uses current examples and a more strategic focus to guide students through the issues and processes associated with managing change.

The Elements of Change website – www.eoc.co.uk/change/articles.shtml
This website includes some very useful articles and case studies on the subject of change. At the time of publication the following were available, free of charge:

- ◆ 'Making Change the Culture – The Initiative in Change Management'

- ◆ 'Business Analysis – Setting the Standard – The Advanced Professional Diploma in Business Analysis in Lloyds TSB'

- ◆ 'People: The Failure in Change – When Will They Ever Learn?'

- ◆ 'The Time for Radical Change'

Full references are provided at the end of the book.

4 Individual and organisational change

One of the main reasons for the failure of change programmes is that managers believe they can control reactions to the change. This theme is about the willingness of individuals and the organisation as a whole to change.

Individuals often have good reason to fear change. In the past change may have meant redundancy, changes to working patterns, changes in status, changes in beliefs and values associated with work. Here we look at how you can change perceptions, how the coping cycle illustrates patterns of behaviour and how forcefield analysis can help you understand individual reactions to change.

When you joined your current organisation, it probably took you some time to find out who mattered if you wanted a decision on something or wanted to lobby for a change. In short, it will have taken you some time to understand the culture of the organisation. The need to change the culture of an organisation as part of the change management process is explored. In this theme we will bring some of the threads about organisational culture together and investigate the nature of an organisation's culture in more depth.

In this theme you will:

◆ **Evaluate the barriers to change represented by the attitudes of individuals**

◆ **Design strategies for reinforcing the forces for change and overcoming those barriers**

◆ **Analyse characteristics of your organisation's current culture**

◆ **Define key characteristics of a desired future culture.**

Changing the individual

Reflect for a moment upon your own reaction to the major changes that have taken place in your personal or business life. Try to remember how you felt immediately after you heard the news. Almost certainly your feelings will have been of unease and worry about how you personally would be affected.

Reactions to change

J Stewart Black (2001) suggests that people don't change easily. He points out, for example, that only one in three people who start an exercise programme follow it through beyond the first couple of weeks. Change isn't easy because people don't see the need for change. They have constructed a mental map of their world which enables them to operate in it relatively successfully. It has worked for them. They tend to stick to what works. Here is an example:

> Ikea, the world's largest furniture company, stuck to a flawed map for a long time. Ikea sells its products in more than 100 countries. When it set up and expanded operations in the US, it did well in all areas except beds and bedding. With poor initial results, executives increased the proportion of marketing and advertising spent on beds, yet sales did not improve.
>
> Unfortunately, these executives had a mental map of the world in which beds were measured using the metric system. While this worked for the rest of the world, in the US the sizes of king, queen and twin reign supreme. Ikea persisted in trying to sell beds and bedding measured in centimetres for nearly three years before finally relenting. Once they changed their map and changed to the US sizing system, sales of beds and bedding improved significantly through the 1990s.

Source: Black (2001)

Black (2001) also points out that even when people recognise the need to change, they don't always change. He suggests the reason is that they don't want to go from being competent in the wrong things to being incompetent in the right things.

Individuals often have good reason to fear change.

Change programmes can bring:

♦ redundancies

♦ change in job content

♦ changes in status, remuneration and benefits

♦ having to work with a new set of people

♦ the requirement to relocate

♦ changes in the beliefs and values associated with your work.

> During the 1990s the big UK clearing banks turned themselves from relatively paternalistic employers into aggressive financial services groups, causing major upheaval for their employees. Within a short space of time the 'jobs for life' culture disappeared and small branch bank managers were turned from pillars of the local community into sellers of financial services.

Before an individual will accept change, there are three conditions to be met. He or she must feel:

1 Dissatisfaction with the existing status quo.

2 That the problems and pain that change will cause are outweighed by the need to change.

3 That the proposed changes are viable.

You may have had experience of a major restructuring at work, where the initial worries were overcome as it was realised that the new organisation would address many of the problems with the current way of working. Specifically, that it would be necessary to suffer some dislocation if things were to improve and that the new organisation and procedures could be made to work.

However, it is not enough for management to know these three conditions have been objectively met for their workforce; the individual workers must feel that the conditions have been met. It is a central role of the change manager to involve the workforce in the change process so that they buy in at this deeper level.

All individuals are different and all will react differently to change. Using an analogy from marketing, it is possible to talk of innovators, early adopters, the early majority, the late majority and laggards – much like the different reactions of consumers to the launch of a new product. Using this analogy, laggards may be viewed as people who resist change.

Other writers refer to innovators and adaptors, distinguishing between people who react to change and those who instigate it. You might like to consider where you would place yourself or colleagues on the innovators–laggards and the innovators–adaptors continuums.

Changing individual perceptions

Kurt Lewin (1952) identified a pattern of freezing, change, and re-freezing to explain the developments over time of an individual's acceptance of a changing environment.

The first stage, freezing, implies a relatively steady state in which there is comparative stability, unchanging routines and a psychological state of relative contentment.

The next stage, moving or change, is characterised by uncertainty, a movement away from what has gone before, but little idea as yet of what future path will be taken. It is a period of instability and experimentation.

The final stage, re-freezing, is back to a period of stability – but stability with different characteristics from the previous period of freezing. The experimentation and stability of the previous period have been resolved, to result in a new direction, new approaches and a period of psychological contentment again.

Source: *Haberberg and Rieple* (2001)

The three-stage process for the individual closely follows that for the organisation. See Figure 4.1.

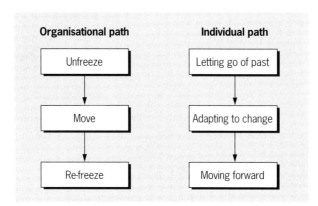

Figure 4.1 *Paths through change*   Source: *Balogun and Hailey* (1999)

Black (2001) suggests that people need to be helped to change their mental models of the world in order to let go of the past. He cites the example of Samsung:

Samsung Electronics is the leading brand of consumer electronic equipment in Korea. It enjoys premium pricing and placement in stores. The head of the company had a problem, however. He could not get senior executives to see that the map that they followed in Korea did not apply in the US. There, brands such as Sony lead the rankings of consumer electronics, not Samsung.

The chief executive helped his executives see the need for change through contrast and confrontation. To be precise, he put them on a plane and they visited important retailers in the US. The contrast of Samsung's premium position in Korea and its bargain basement image in the US was made abundantly clear as the group went from store to store and saw their products not front and centre but often placed in bargain bins. This experience changed their thinking.

Source: *Black* (2001)

The coping cycle

There are various models of how people come to accept change over time. One such is the coping cycle. See Table 4.1.

Stage 1	Denial	'We have always done things this way'
		'Why change, we are making a profit aren't we?'
		'Don't change a winning team'
		'We tried that before but it did not work'
Stage 2	Defence	Reality intrudes and people realise they must react.
		'That's fine but it won't work in my area'
		'I'd like to get involved but I have too much work to do'
		'The theory is fine, but it won't work in practice'
Stage 3	Discarding	'Whether I like it or not, it is going to happen, so I had better...'
		'Well here it is; we are committed to it; here's how I see it'
		'I was giving that new machine a try, and do you know...?'
		'I've been asked to join the group looking at x'
Stage 4	Adaptation	'We are still trying to get the new x to work'
		'We are getting most of the output from the new x but I still think we need to...'
		'We are never going to get x to work unless those so and sos in that department pull their finger out'
		'I kept telling them that that was what we needed to do and finally they have done it'
Stage 5	Internalisation	What was the future state is now the current state.
		'I was talking to x in the y department the other day about that customer order...'
		'We are getting a group together to see whether we want to implement that software upgrade'
		'That is one of the things I want to raise at my next review'

Table 4.1 *The coping cycle*   Source: *Carnall* (1999)

This coping cycle for the individual is an important element of any change management process and in many ways is central. See Figure 4.2.

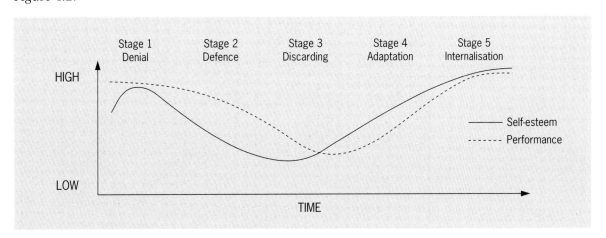

Figure 4.2 *The coping cycle: effects on performance and self-esteem*

Source: *Carnall* (1999)

When you contribute to change management programmes you will need to recognise that both performance and self-esteem are likely to drop during the early stages of the programme. In a successful change programme, as the programme progresses the workforce may feel a tremendous sense of liberation as their ideas and potential contribution to the organisation are recognised for the first time. In a virtuous circle, shown in Figure 4.3, this steep rise in self-esteem can lead to improved performance and speed of implementation.

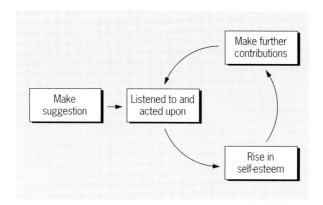

Figure 4.3 *Virtuous circle – self-esteem leading to improved performance*

Forcefield analysis

To conclude this section we will look at an example of the forces that may be influential in encouraging an individual to consider or welcome change. Kurt Lewin in 1952 developed a way of analysing these forces using what he called forcefield analysis. See Figure 4.4.

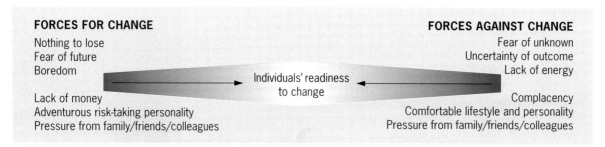

Figure 4.4 *Forcefield of factors influencing individual change*

Source: *Haberberg and Rieple* (2001)

Individuals value a strong element of stability and predictability in their lives. They are naturally fearful of change and will oppose it unless they see good reason to change.

It is your task as a change manager to reinforce the forces for change and address the forces against change. Hence, a programme to increase efficiency may be sold on the basis that without it the organisation has no future in an increasingly competitive world; here fear of the unknown will be replaced by a feeling that the employee has nothing to lose.

Any change programme has to be managed with sensitivity, both to the needs of the ongoing business and also to the needs of the individual. This was no different for Secure Components.

Neil knew that ultimately change was about people. He recognised that the people intimately and personally affected by change may not share the same enthusiasm for change as either senior management or the change manager!

He had been on the receiving end of a change programme earlier in his career and empathised with people's personal and very real concerns. Insensitivity to these concerns, ignoring them and hoping they will go away, is a strategy for likely failure. Neil needed to prepare for a range of likely reactions.

Neil's approach was simple. He planned to adopt an open and honest, non-confrontational communication style. He would reinforce the need for change with credible argument supported by the reality of the internal and external analyses, and personalise this as appropriate. He would also reassure concerns about the positive and personal consequences of change and, as appropriate, contrast with the likely negative consequences of denying change.

Neil brainstormed typical concerns that were likely to be raised, and simply developed a range of responses that would reassure people, reinforce the need for change and which were very consistent with both the vision of the future and the change framework. This would help reduce concerns, but for Neil the process of adapting to change was insufficient to achieve the essence of the change programme.

Neil believed that the vital key to this change programme was wide participation and, importantly, participation in empowered teams. Through participation, involvement would be facilitated, through empowerment, real ownership would be established and through teamwork, mutual support and improved communication would be achieved.

Ask yourself:

◆ *How would Neil's plans help people through each stage of the coping strategy?*

◆ *In what ways might company performance be improved by increasing worker participation and empowerment?*

Activity 10
Changing the individual

Objectives

Completing this activity will help you to:

◆ evaluate the barriers to change represented by the attitudes of individuals

◆ design strategies for reinforcing the forces for change and overcoming those barriers.

Case study

Read the short case study below.

The effects of changes in the Queensland hospital system

In recent years, governments have actively pursued reforms of the Australian public sector. A main objective of health sector reform has been to reduce hospital waiting lists and increase the overall level of efficiency of the public hospital system. This is in a context of high demand for hospital services, an ageing population, new medical technologies and treatments, and a growing community expectation for the provision of the most advanced care available. In one Queensland hospital over a year, there was a 16 per cent increase in the number of theatre cases and admissions. The average daily number of inpatients increased by 6 per cent, the occupancy rate increased from 86 to 92 per cent and the average length of stay fell by 14 per cent.

Yet the government allocated only limited funds to achieve this. These changes had to be achieved without increases in staff levels or salaries, and inevitably this burden fell on individual members of staff. One of the major effects of these increases in work intensity was a decline in staffing well-being and morale. Increases in demand for counselling for stress-related issues, high staff turnover and absenteeism levels were seen. Periodically the strain also showed in the form of industrial disputes, although the underlying professionalism of health workers restrained the kinds and extent of industrial action pursued; striking was still perceived as unprofessional and unethical.

Source: *Cameron* (1998) *quoted by Haberberg and Rieple* (2001)

Task

Using the forcefield framework below, analyse the forces for and against change in the Queensland hospital system and consider their relative strengths. Then ask how could:

◆ the forces against change be countered?

◆ the forces for change be reinforced?

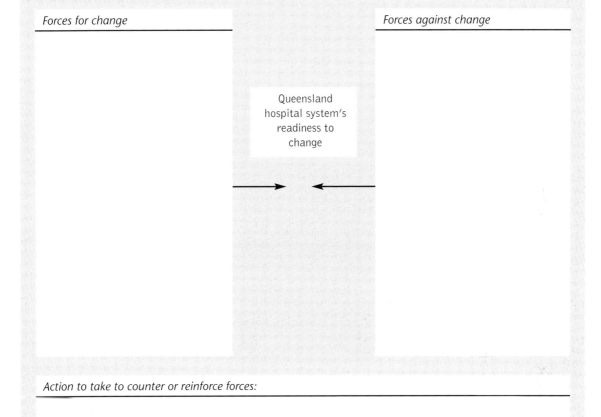

Action to take to counter or reinforce forces:

Feedback

Increased expectations from public services and the introduction of targets are common across many countries. Many workers will have gone into these public services out of a desire to serve the public away from what they see as the profit-orientated private sector. To have their performance measured can seem like a criticism of what they try to do and of their commitment to the service.

79

The forces against change might therefore include:

◆ a feeling that their public service ethos was under attack

◆ a distrust of new performance measures, where previously the only yardstick might have been the opinion of professional colleagues

◆ an identification with the existing culture of the hospital, which for many would provide a social as well as a work focus for their lives

◆ strong identification with fellow workers in the hospital might lead to decisions to 'fight this together'.

Against this would be forces in favour of change, possibly:

◆ a feeling that 'things cannot go on as they are'

◆ frustration with current promotion prospects

◆ lack of outlet for the individual's creativity

◆ public dissatisfaction with the performance of the health services would also effect the individual and increase the desire to regain public confidence.

Changing the culture

This is not the place to join the debate about the true nature of culture, but here are some definitions:

The deeper level of basic assumptions and beliefs that are shared by members of an organisation, that operate unconsciously and define in a basic 'taken for granted' fashion an organisation's view of itself and its environment.

Source: *Schein* (1992)

Organisational culture is not just another piece of the puzzle. From our point of view, a culture is not something an organisation has: a culture is something an organisation is.

Source: *Pacanowsky and O'Donnell-Trujillo* (1982)

Pacanowsky and O'Donnell-Trujillo probably overstate their case, but certainly culture is something at the core of an organisation's being.

Shared meaning, shared understanding and shared sense making are all different ways of describing culture. In talking about culture we are really talking about a process of reality construction that allows people to see and understand particular events, actions, objects, utterances, or situations in distinctive ways. These patterns of understanding also provide a basis for naming one's own behaviour sensible and meaningful.

Source: *Senior* (1997)

Analysing the culture

A widely used tool for analysing the culture of an organisation is the cultural web devised by Gerry Johnson. The web consists of different elements which interact to form the cultural paradigm or mindset of the organisation. The paradigm is the predominant mental model that people share of the organisation – characterised by the phrase, 'the way we do things here'. See Figure 4.5.

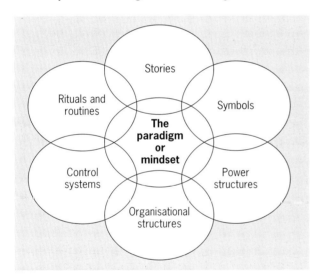

Figure 4.5 *The cultural web*   Source: *Johnson and Scholes* (1999)

Table 4.2 gives the different elements of the web Johnson identifies. Alongside are given his examples drawn from the experiences of the National Health Service (NHS), the UK's public provider of hospital care.

Elements	Examples from the NHS in the 1990s
The *routine* ways that members of the organisation behave towards each other, and towards those outside the organisation, make up 'the way we do things around here'	Doctors have traditionally taken it for granted that they know best. How will they feel about programmes that attempt to involve patients in their own care?
The *rituals* of the organisation are the special events through which the organisation emphasises what is particularly important and reinforces 'the way we do things around here'	In the NHS there have been numerous rituals to ensure that 'everyone knows their place'. These include the elevation of clinicians with ritual consultation ceremonies and ward rounds
The *stories* told by members of the organisation to each other, to outsiders, to new recruits and so on, embed the present in its organisational history and also flag up important events and personalities	The heroes of the health service are in curing, not in caring. The system considered itself under attack in 1994 and there were many tales of villainous politicians faced by heroic medical staff
Symbols such as logos, offices, cars and titles, or the type of language and terminology commonly used, become a shorthand representation of the nature of the organisation	In major teaching hospitals in the UK, consultants described patients as 'clinical material', showing a distancing from the emotional side of medical care. There are numerous examples of dress code for doctors, nurses, auxiliary staff, etc.
Power structures are closely associated with the paradigm of an organisation, with those in positions of power sharing the core belief systems of the organisation	Historically, senior clinicians were the most powerful figures and managers seen as 'administrators'. Powerful informal networks existed to press for resources and resist change

Table 4.2 *Example of the cultural web*

Source: *Adapted from Johnson and Scholes* (1999)

Important though it is to analyse the culture of the organisation, it is your ability to change the culture so that it better supports the organisation's objectives that really matters; to change the organisation, the culture of the organisation must also change. As we shall see below, to a great extent the new culture will evolve during the change process, but it is still useful to create a vision of what the changed culture might look like.

Changing the organisation's culture

A number of writers provide lists of the characteristics that go to make up an organisation's culture. You could use these lists, summarised in Table 4.3, to analyse the current culture and prepare a vision of the new culture.

Member identity	The degree to which employees identify with the organisation as a whole rather than with their type of job or field of professional expertise
Group emphasis	The degree to which work activities are organised around groups rather than individuals
People focus	The degree to which management decisions take into consideration the effect of outcomes on people within the organisation
Unit integration	The degree to which units within the organisation are encouraged to operate in a co-ordinated or interdependent manner
Control	The degree to which rules, regulations and direct supervision are used to oversee and control employee behaviour
Risk tolerance	The degree to which employees are encouraged to be aggressive, innovative and risk-seeking
Reward criteria	The degree to which rewards such as salary increases and promotions are allocated according to employee performance rather than seniority, favouritism or other non-performance factors
Conflict tolerance	The degree to which employees are encouraged to air conflicts and criticisms openly
Means-ends orientation	The degree to which management focuses on results or outcomes rather than on the techniques and processes used to achieve those outcomes
Open-system focus	The degree to which the organisation monitors and responds to changes in the external environment

Table 4.3 *The characteristics of organisational culture*

Source: *Robbins* (1993)

The list of characteristics of an organisation's culture prepared by Robbins and shown here provides such a basis for action. Take some of the headings and start to think through how they apply to your own organisation.

If you are contributing to a change management programme in an organisation that has an established culture, then the following options are available to you:

1 Manage around the culture.

2 Try to change the culture to fit the strategy.

3 Change the strategy to fit the culture.

4 Ignore the culture.

For transformational programmes the first option is unlikely to be practical. New ways of delivering health care in the UK's National Health Service cannot be developed without changing the attitudes of medical staff.

The second option of consciously trying to change the culture also rarely works in practice. Organisations exist for a purpose, and the culture ultimately exists in order to deliver the organisation's outputs. It is very difficult to change culture if no link is made to the organisation's outputs and the processes by which those outputs are delivered. You may have experience of quality and excellence programmes which seemed to gain a life of their own, divorced from the realities of providing the customer with a better product or delivering a better service.

Changing the strategy to fit the culture might appear defeatist but it is right to consider the strengths and weaknesses of an organisation's culture before deciding on the direction an organisation will take.

> In the 1980s the UK telecommunications giant, BT, attempted to transform itself from a government department to a commercial company. In doing so, it made redundant large numbers of its personnel, including older and more experienced members of staff. It found itself hiring back many of these staff as consultants as they had an essential understanding of how to operate the business in many areas.

Surprisingly, the final option of ignoring the culture may be the best option, or at least in terms of making explicit the desire to change the culture. Using this approach, you will concentrate on the new outputs required and let the culture evolve to meet the new performance requirements. This is not to say that you can just sit back; your job is to involve the workforce so that they become enthusiastic participants in the change process with the new culture forming through the interactions of people during the transition stage.

The learning organisation

The learning organisation is not about increasing the number of training days. Different definitions and perspectives have been taken by different writers, but we can take the key elements of a learning organisation to be:

- ◆ embedding learning into the culture of the organisation so that it becomes a key element of the 'way of doing things around here'
- ◆ defining learning in a broad way, encompassing learning from experience and being open to new knowledge and ideas
- ◆ seeing learning as a creative process enabling people to develop new and expansive patterns of thinking
- ◆ nurturing learning as a means of constantly transforming the organisation.

> **I also remember talking with a senior manager in a diversified group who had introduced computerised photo-composition for a newspaper company in the early 1970s. The company had allowed the typesetters to try out the visual display units in a test room but not in a training environment. Providing support, they avoided any sense of formal training and were surprised to find that, allowed to learn at their own pace, the typesetters embraced the technology enthusiastically and quickly.**
>
> **Carnall (1999)**

Some commentators argue that an organisation's most sure source of sustainable competitive advantage is its ability to continually question whether its norms are still valid or whether there are better ways of doing business. The willingness to modify behaviour to reflect new knowledge and insights is at the heart of the concept of the learning organisation.

Organisational learning is applicable to managing the transition stage of the change management process. Its stress upon the need to monitor the activities of the organisation so as to provide feedback for improved performance is a central technique in developing the new organisation and its culture during the transitional stage.

Neil did not know how to change the company culture, but he knew that it would be key to the success of his change programme. He formed a picture in his mind of the key cultural features that he would like to see and developed strong linkages with the vision and objectives of the change programme.

He would use performance management techniques to reinforce positive behaviour towards the key cultural dimensions, and to discourage behaviour that was inconsistent with the key cultural dimensions. Put another way, the workforce would become accustomed to having the new culture as the yardstick against which the acceptability of actions and decisions would be judged.

The key cultural dimensions that Neil needed to establish were:

a   Customer focus and customer satisfaction.

b   Cross-functional team working and effective communications.

c   Empowerment and responsibility.

These three concepts were alien to the organisation at the start of the change programme, but Neil argued that internalisation of these three key cultural concepts would then enable the organisation to redefine its wider cultural framework and align with those concepts.

Neil spent a considerable amount of time continually challenging, reinforcing, influencing and selling the vision and the change programme strategy until it became second nature to everyone in the organisation. He made great efforts to link the successes of the change programme to the new culture and vision. This process continued throughout the whole period of change, continually reinforcing positives and discouraging negatives.

Ask yourself:

◆ *What tools were available to change the organisational culture?*

◆ *How can cultural change be internalised?*

Activity 11
Changing the culture

Objectives

Use this activity to:

♦ analyse characteristics of your organisation's current culture

♦ define key characteristics of a desired future culture.

Task

In this activity you will examine your organisation's cultural characteristics as defined by Robbins (1993).

1 Put a cross on each scale according to how you rate your organisation. For example, if the members of your organisation identify most strongly with their organisation rather than their type of job or field of professional expertise, then place your cross closer to the organisation end of the line.

2 Think about what may be holding your organisation back and what you would wish to see changed. Using a different coloured pen, place a cross where you would wish to see the organisation rated in the future.

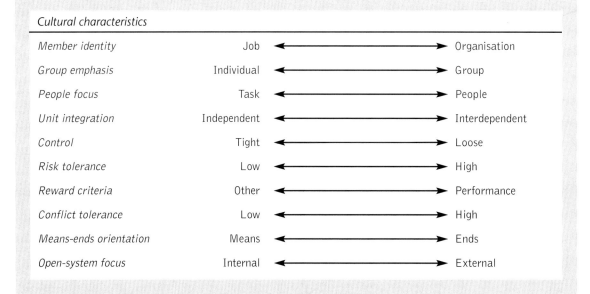

Cultural characteristics			
Member identity	Job	←————————→	Organisation
Group emphasis	Individual	←————————→	Group
People focus	Task	←————————→	People
Unit integration	Independent	←————————→	Interdependent
Control	Tight	←————————→	Loose
Risk tolerance	Low	←————————→	High
Reward criteria	Other	←————————→	Performance
Conflict tolerance	Low	←————————→	High
Means-ends orientation	Means	←————————→	Ends
Open-system focus	Internal	←————————→	External

Source: *Adapted from Robbins* (1993)

Feedback

Your results will obviously depend upon the culture of your organisation. If you put most of your crosses closer to the left-hand side, then your organisation is most probably ripe for change, but that change will be the more difficult to manage.

In your vision of a future culture, your crosses should have been closer to the right-hand side, stressing teamworking, flexibility, comfort with an unregulated environment and an external, customer focus.

To conclude this activity, go back and mark in order of importance the three characteristics that you think it is most important to change.

◆ Recap

This theme examines change from the perspective of individuals and the organisation as a whole.

Evaluate the barriers to change represented by the attitudes of individuals

◆ Individuals often have good reason to fear change. Before an individual will accept change they must feel: dissatisfaction with the status quo; that the problems caused by the change will be outweighed by the need to change; and that the proposed changes are viable.

◆ The coping cycle is a useful framework within which to evaluate your own and others' reactions to change.

Design strategies for reinforcing the forces for change and overcoming those barriers

◆ When deciding how to start a change management programme, you will need to address the issue of how change affects the individual. A forcefield analysis provides a framework.

Analyse characteristics of your organisation's current culture

◆ The culture of an organisation can be analysed or described in many ways. It is necessary to describe your organisation's current culture as a basis for saying what it is you wish to change and what the new culture should look like.

◆ A cultural web can provide a view of the organisation's culture and a list of characteristics that make up that culture.

Define key characteristics of a desired future culture

◆ It is useful to find a set of characteristics that match your organisation's desired vision to provide the fundamentals of the future culture.

◆ We have explored Robbins' (1993) list of cultural characteristics as a benchmark.

▶▶ More @

Balogun, J., Hailey, V. H., Johnson, G. and Scholes, K. (2003) 2nd edition, *Exploring Strategic Change*, Financial Times Prentice Hall
Exploring Strategic Change focuses on the implementation of organisational change and the management of organisational transitions. It seeks to move beyond the formulation of strategy by taking the planning stage through to implementation. The text examines the change process from analysis of context and the diagnosis of needs through the stages of transition and transference to practical change.

Campbell, D., Stonehouse, G. and Houston, B. (2002) 2nd edition, *Business Strategy: an Introduction*, Elsevier Butterworth-Heinemann
This is an accessible textbook that provides a straightforward and comprehensive guide to complex issues and concepts. See in particular Chapter 3 'Human resources and culture' and Chapter 10 'Strategic implementation'.

To find out more about the concept and practice of **learning organisations** you could use the Internet:

◆ Research the work of the following experts: Chris Argyris – see, for example, infed.org (part of the UK National Grid for Learning) at www.infed.org/thinkers/argyris.htm – and Donald Schön

◆ Try Business.com, the business-focused search engine and directory, at www.business.com/directory/management and search for articles on learning organisations

◆ The article 'A Learning-Based Approach To Organizational Change' is available from the Society for Organizational Learning at www.solonline.org/repository/download/ OLC%20STUDY***.%20Rev.OD.doc?item_id=360596

Mind Tools – www.mindtools.com/forcefld.html
Try the article 'Force Field Analysis – Understanding The Pressures For and Against Change'

Full references are provided at the end of the book.

5 Techniques for sustainable change

Successful change management programmes require momentum, enthusiasm and a clear signal that things will never be the same again. A successful launch will provide a firm foundation and will make these requirements much easier to achieve. This theme examines the ways we can move from the launch of a change programme through styles of management appropriate for a change environment to the creation of an organisational culture that thrives on change.

What style of management is appropriate during the transition to the new organisations we are trying to create? Certainly we know that there is no one right way to manage the change programme – what is appropriate for one organisation may be entirely wrong for another. Current management styles can be used but these are more likely to be suited to ongoing operations than in a period when everything is in flux. Moreover, one of the objectives of the change programme will probably be to introduce new management styles and these need to evolve as part of the change programme.

In the same way as there is no single best approach to change management programmes, different management styles will be needed for the different groups, or stakeholders, involved in each change management programme. Here we explore ways of tailoring the management of the change programme to the needs of these different groups.

Finally we look at the dynamics of the ways in which organisations change. Setting up the change management project in the right way can create, a virtuous circle, with inputs from stakeholders leading to positive reassessments of the programme, leading to increased enthusiasm for the programme's development.

In this theme you will:

◆ **Identify possible launch strategies**

◆ **Consider how different styles of managing change may be appropriate in different contexts**

◆ **Evaluate different approaches for different target groups within an organisation**

◆ **Explore the importance of organisational dynamics in the change process and how to sustain a culture of change for the future.**

Launch strategies

When you contribute to a change management programme, you need to ensure that the launch declares to employees and perhaps the world that the organisation is permanently changing the way it does business. A successful launch shows that change is possible, builds momentum for the transition period and shows the possibilities of a better tomorrow.

Ideally, the launch should take the workforce past the point of no return so that they leave their comfort zone and are forced to embark on the transition process. Usually, however, this is not possible right at the start of the project and will take place during one of the later building blocks of the change programme.

The launch should provide growing confidence in the organisation, the change team and in the individual member of staff. If you get this right, it can then lead to a virtuous circle (see Figure 5.1) where, by demonstrating that change is possible, people know they can make a difference and therefore start providing numerous ideas of their own that have been repressed in the past.

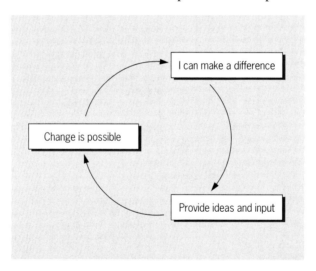

Figure 5.1 *A virtuous circle for change*

The importance of completion

Black (2001) argues that one reason why change fails is because people tire of their efforts to change, get disappointing early results and revert back to their old mental models. Early success in small ways is important to provide positive reinforcement. The change manager has a key role in creating commitment to carry through the change from launch to completion.

Alternative launch strategies

If your organisation has carried out a number of change management initiatives in the past, there may be a great deal of cynicism about the possibility of change. It can be argued that the first mistake in launching, say, a total quality management (TQM) programme is to say that you are going to launch a TQM programme. It might be better to concentrate on the outputs from the change programme and introduce elements of TQM along the way.

You may also encounter resistance from a variety of other sources, materialising as arrogance, complacency or fear. You will need to discover the source of the resistance as part of the analysis stage and tailor the launch strategy accordingly. For instance, if there is arrogance as to the technical prowess of the organisation, then it might be possible to buy in or outsource some process which is superior to that produced in-house. Where there is fear of redundancies, then that can be addressed directly through pledges of no redundancies coupled with events to stress the management's confidence in the workforce and the organisation's future.

Defining the change

Rosabeth Moss Kanter argues that the way in which a change project is defined affects its acceptability to those who are going to be affected. She advises change agents to define their projects in ways that make them sound:

Viable

The change should appear capable of being subjected to a pilot before going the whole way

Reversible

Convince your audience that what you are proposing can be changed back to the status quo if it falls to pieces – irreversible changes are seen as risky

Divisible

Where the change has a number of separate dimensions, present these as potentially independent aspects of a broader change programme – so when single issues cause problems the whole package doesn't have to fold

Concrete

Make the changes and their outcomes tangible and avoid expressing what will happen in abstract and general terms, which do not convey an accurate feel for the proposals

Familiar

Make proposals in terms that other people in the organisation can recognise, because if what you propose is so far over the horizon people can't recognise it, they'll feel out of their comfort zones and start resisting

Congruent
Proposals for change should wherever possible be seen to fit with the rest of the organisation and be consistent with existing policy and practice

Sexy
Choose projects that have publicity value – in terms of external or media relations, or in terms of internal politics – what will the local press go for; what will excite the chief executive?

Source: *Based on Kanter* (1983) *quoted by Huczynski and Buchanan* (1991)

Depending on the characteristics of the particular project you have in hand, you may not agree that all the features suggested by Kanter in 'Defining the change' are desirable. For instance, by making the whole project viable, reversible and divisible, you may be giving the message that change is not inevitable, that we can always go back to the way things were if people do not like this new approach. Over the trial period, the groups against change may be given a chance to marshal their forces.

The last four features are more generally applicable. It is essential that participants grasp what the change management programme is all about.

Selecting the launch team

The manager leading the change management team will not always be able to get the individual people they want but great care needs to be taken in the composition of the launch team.

The ultimate aim of the programme will be to involve everyone in the organisation but the membership and individual actions of the launch team can send important signals. A successful launch is an opportunity to show that there is kudos to being associated with the changes being made.

It is normally a good idea to include representatives from different areas of the organisation but the need to recruit the most suitable people may mean that this is not possible. One tactic used by change managers is to include a well-known cynic on the team so as to demonstrate the possibility of changing individual attitudes – obviously there are dangers with this!

Neil set out to ensure that the change programme would be launched successfully and that growing confidence levels would encourage people to take the change programme on to bigger and better things.

He knew that any launch strategy needed to be sensitive to people's needs. One launch strategy will work in one organisation but not in another. This is a pure judgement call, and is best bounced off key stakeholders before implementation.

Neil decided to make a major and clear statement that this change programme was going to be like no other that the company had ever experienced. This one was going to go off with a bang, and was going to be successful because there would be no turning back.

Neil gained agreement to address the fundamental issue of cross-functional teamwork and communications, and engineer a total factory rearrangement into operational cells. Everybody affected by this change was briefed, key stakeholders were involved in special workshops designed to make them think about how the new arrangement would work and a daily 'countdown to transformation' was highlighted on numerous company notice boards.

The company's experience of previous projects was as chequered as its experience with change programmes. There was always a lot of talk about changing things, but something always came up and the plan was soon forgotten. Neil was not going to let that happen. He assembled a team of engineers and planned the relocation to the last detail, with contingency plans for the more risky parts of the plan. Neil planned for success. A successful factory rearrangement was imperative to the future success of the change programme. Failure was not an option.

Even with all the communication and involvement, many believed that it would never happen. Neil recalls: 'Thursday evening, they all went home, Tuesday morning, they all returned to work. After months of briefings, communications and their involvement throughout, they were dumbstruck by what greeted them that morning. The whole factory had been rearranged and it took over an hour for it to sink in that the change programme was not only going to happen, it had just started.'

Ask yourself:

♦ *How important was the success of the symbolic factory rearrangement?*

♦ *What are the likely consequences of a symbolic failure at the launch stage?*

Activity 12
Designing the programme

Objectives

Use this activity to:

♦ design key features of a change programme

♦ evaluate a proposed change programme against key criteria.

Task

Kanter (1983) argues that the way in which a change project is defined affects its acceptability to management and the workforce.

Using her checklist below, take a specific project, not necessarily a change programme, with which you have been involved and say whether it had the features listed.

If the project did not have these features, was this a problem?

Change programme:

Feature	Did it have this feature? Y	N	Comment
Viable	☐	☐	
Reversible	☐	☐	
Divisible	☐	☐	
Concrete	☐	☐	
Familiar	☐	☐	
Congruent	☐	☐	
Sexy	☐	☐	

Source: *Based on Kanter* (1983)

Feedback

You were asked to evaluate a project with which you have been involved against these criteria. For a project that has well-defined boundaries, say the implementation of a new software package, a remuneration scheme or the launch of a new product, the features viable, reversible and divisible are likely to be highly desirable. The features concrete, familiar and congruent are likely to be fairly easily attainable. The project is unlikely to be sexy, but then this is not really a problem.

The situation may be very different for a major change programme. The first three characteristics may be undesirable in that management wants to signal transformational change where there is no going back to previous practice. To make the proposals concrete, familiar and congruent may be a major challenge as the organisation moves into new territory. To generate motivation and build the positive forces for change, the programme needs an exciting image.

Styles of managing change

You may be in the process of developing your own style of management. Broadly, the choice of management style lies on a continuum from coercion to democracy. Different writers provide different classifications but the main types are outlined in Table 5.1.

Style	Features	Objectives
Democratic	Use small group briefings to provide information and discuss issues	The aim is to reach a consensus on what is to be done
Collaboration	Senior management has already decided in outline what is to change. Employees provide input into how change is to be effected and how it is to be achieved	The aim is to achieve commitment and ownership by the workforce within the framework laid down by management
Participation	Employees consulted on the how of the implementation. They may have limited decision ability on the details of the how	The aim is to achieve the commitment of the workforce while leaving them limited discretion over what happens
Direction	Change leaders make the majority of decisions about what to change and how. Use of authority to direct change	To sell change to the workforce
Coercion	Use of power to impose change	To use the workforce to achieve the end result

Table 5.1 *Styles of managing change*

Think about which one of these styles is most prevalent in your own organisation and which fits your own style of management. This current management style of the organisation may be inappropriate both for the transition period and the future state of the organisation.

> The command and control style of management which existed in the old national telecommunications companies was rendered inappropriate not only by privatisation but also by rapid advances in technology, which broke down the barriers between companies and opened up new sources of competition. To respond to these upheavals in the environment, management needed to develop new management styles, both to implement the change programme itself and to conduct business in the more fluid, competitive future business environment. The implementation of a more open style of management was therefore part of the change process itself.

Every style of management has its own advantages and disadvantages. Using Table 5.2, think about the situations in which an individual style would be most appropriate.

Style	Advantages	Disadvantages
Democratic	Ensures equality of availability of information and influence on decisions	May not convince everyone of the need to change. Likely to be very time-consuming and support may not be translated into action
Collaboration	Spreads support and ownership of change by increasing levels of involvement. Often good when dealing with professionals	Time-consuming. Little control over decisions made. May lead to changes which management find unacceptable
Participation/ intervention	Again, spreads ownership and support for change, but within a more controlled framework. Easier to shape decisions	Can be perceived as manipulation
Direction	Less time-consuming. Provides a clear change of direction and focus	Potentially less support and commitment, and therefore proposed changes may be resisted
Coercion	Allows for prompt action	Unlikely to achieve buy-in without a crisis

Table 5.2 *Advantages and disadvantages of management styles*

The organisational context

Your choice of style depends, as we have seen, on the context. Your choice of style during the transition phase will be influenced by such factors as:

- ◆ The amount of time your organisation has – if the organisation is facing meltdown, strong central direction may be the only option.
- ◆ The nature of your workforce – highly skilled workforces may demand to be consulted.

◆ The nature of the organisation's products – in consultancy practices, the product is most often developed by the management consultants as they carry out projects for clients. Here a democratic approach may be the only option.

Neil knew he must adopt a management style that was appropriate to what needed to be accomplished. At Secure Components, Neil had to both sell the recommended strategic option to senior management and obtain management buy-in. This stage required a predominantly democratic/collaborative approach.

During the factory rearrangement, a more directive style was adopted. However, following the rearrangement, Neil's management style gradually but progressively developed from predominantly directive through to predominantly collaborative. At the start, the directive style was necessary to provide a clear direction for change but this soon became a collaborative style as empowered improvement teams started to form and perform.

It was important to move to a more collaborative style at the earliest opportunity because this style was more consistent with the key cultural dimensions that needed to be achieved. This style was encapsulated within the vision and change objectives, and it was important that Neil 'walked the talk' so that this style was judged positively as evidence that things were changing.

Colleagues were surprised that during this period of rapid change the predominantly collaborative style was not necessarily time-consuming. In addition, with appropriate supportive facilitation, the empowered teams' activities did not lose sight of the direction of change and the underlying objectives.

The teams were very excited to become engaged in the change programme. They found the collaborative style very refreshing, but initially did not understand how to react. They had been raised on directive, perhaps part-coercive, style and needed some time to build their confidence to engage in this new style of working.

As the change programme developed, Neil found that the need to adopt a directive style became much less frequent. This indicated to Neil that the empowered teams were starting to understand the new game rules and were relishing the opportunity to learn, experiment and improve the way they conducted business. They were learning to work smarter.

Ask yourself:
◆ *Why are different styles appropriate at different stages of a change programme?*
◆ *How appropriate are the styles used during the period of rapid change to the future running of the company?*

Activity 13
Choices of style

Objectives

Use this activity to:

◆ consider how different styles of implementing change may be appropriate in different contexts

◆ target change at different sections of the workforce

◆ formulate recommendations as to which is the best alternative.

This task is based on a case study on the change programme at KPMG, the large international firm of accountants and consultants. The company initiated a change in 1992 to differentiate itself from other accountancy firms.

Case study

Read the following case study.

Initiating strategic change at KPMG

KPMG is a large international firm of accountants and consultants. Like many other such organisations, traditionally the primary interface to the market had been discipline-based practice units (audit, tax, consultancy). At the beginning of the 1990s Colin Sharman, partner in charge of the south-east region, perceived the need to change the firm into a client-focused organisation. Although the firm was increasingly run along corporate lines, each partner of the firm is, in effect, an owner-manager, and has to agree, or at least not disagree, with any change. Given this partnership structure, and the fact that the firm was very successful in its existing form, Sharman had no mandate or authority to impose change. He initiated change in a way designed to obtain the support needed from the critical mass of partners.

As a first step, a series of partner workshops were run, at which the partners considered the firm's strategy, the blockages to change and the actions needed. Sharman attended briefing sessions at the end of each workshop, but did not direct the outcomes from the workshops. Subsequently, Sharman held evening feedback sessions attended by most of the partners, which were focused on building consensus on the need for change and what should be done. The senior managers' conference was also used as a way of getting those below the level of partner involved. The senior managers were asked to work through a similar process to that undertaken at the workshops by the partners. This was followed by more briefing meetings for partners and senior managers.

In 1992, a special partners' conference was called where the 20:20 Vision, the blueprint for change, was presented to give impetus to the change process. Similar events were held for both senior and junior managers. Change was also communicated in a variety of other ways, including videos, glossy brochures, personal repetition by Colin Sharman, and later on publicly, through sections of the media.

Source: *Balogun and Hailey* (1999)

Task

Now answer the following questions:

1 Why did Sharman decide to target the various sections of the workforce differently?

2 Do you think there were dangers in the approach adopted? If so, what were they?

Feedback

Colin Sharman had no power to impose change. He could only put in place interventions to trigger questioning and challenging of the status quo. A number of interventions were used, such as workshops, conferences and feedback. However, the style of change was different for different groups of staff. For the partners, Sharman put in place extensive collaboration. For the senior managers, their opinions were sought, but at a later stage, so the style for them was more like participation. Those below senior manager level were never really consulted at all. They were informed of the decisions, and as such, the change style for them was direction.

The danger here is that the workforce may feel threatened by changes in which they have had no input. For an organisation employing so many professionally qualified staff, there is the likelihood that they will feel undervalued because their opinions have not been sought. Senior managers must gain the commitment of this group.

Targeting change

Organisations are made up of the formal structure and informal groups. The formal structure is that laid down in the company's organisation chart, procedures and job descriptions. The informal structure may be very much more powerful in terms of influencing change; it is here that the culture is most firmly embedded, power exercised and control maintained.

If you are to be effective as a change manager, you need to be attuned to this informal structure. You should design the detail of the change management process both to use the informal structure where it gives the organisation potential strength and to change it where it represents a barrier. Different considerations will apply to senior management, middle management and the workforce.

It is important to work very closely with senior management. They provide the change management team with its terms of reference and formal authority. From within the ranks of senior management must be the champions and protectors of the change process, ready to deal with the political issues, promote the project and help remove barriers to change. At the same time, senior management need to feel that the change manager is representing them, is presenting them in a favourable light to the workforce and is not abusing their trust.

If a change management process fails, it is most likely to be with middle management; they generally have most to lose and least to gain. They will already be under pressure and will initially see the change proposals in negative terms. They are also more used to being measured by short-term, internal performance measures and may be unsettled by the more fluid style of management required during the period of flux. Change programmes are often about empowering the workforce, but where does this leave middle management? They must be persuaded that there will be plenty of scope for building a career after the programme and that proving abilities during the transition process will build their credibility. Middle management need to feel that they are still in control during the transition period and must be fully involved as members of the different steering groups and working parties.

The workforce may feel a great sense of liberation during the change management process. They may feel that for the first time their views are being noted and that they have a contribution to make. The temptation all the time during the change process is for middle management to continue managing at the micro-level; this will kill the workforce's new-found energy and commitment. This is a period to take risks and allow the workforce discretion and control. What is perhaps most difficult is to maintain this new way of doing things once the change management process is over and it is time to re-freeze the organisation.

Change the person?

Symbolic changes at Siemens
In the mid-1990s, the 150-year-old German conglomerate faced increased competition and needed to improve its speed of response and innovation. Heinrich von Pierer, Siemens' CEO, responded by challenging some of the firm's deeply held beliefs. He started talking of 'tearing down barriers within the company', creating a 'climate for honest open dialogue' and 'optimising entire process chains', which was a contrast to the firm's normal language. He also introduced a company-wide process improvement programme called ToP (Time-optimised Processes) which aimed to improve growth, profitability and innovation. But whereas in the old days everything would have been organised centrally, each business unit was now responsible for bringing about its own change.

Von Pierer also sought a clearer market orientation for the company's R&D, to bring together technology push and market pull approaches. Previously Siemens had not particularly looked elsewhere for guidance, but it now started to benchmark itself against its competitors and studied retailers and financial services to improve its own logistics and customer service. Von

> Pierer put more emphasis on profitability, creating some 250 independent and entrepreneurial business units. Employees were to be paid by results rather than by seniority, and staff members were expected to assess their superiors as well as being assessed by them. Siemens also planned to introduce a stock-options scheme for its directors – a relative novelty in Germany. Senior management positions are now only open to those with international experience.

Source: *Haberberg and Rieple* (2001)

Change management programmes are undertaken in order to achieve the strategic goals of an organisation. For a company this will usually mean maximising shareholder value through generating profits and building a strong, growing business. In order to achieve these strategic goals, what exactly is it that we are attempting to change? Do we need to:

- ◆ change employees' beliefs and values?
- ◆ change the behaviour of our employees?
- ◆ concentrate on changing the employees' outputs?

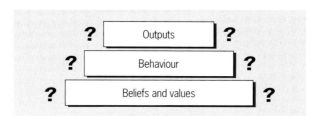

Figure 5.2 *Targeting individual change*

We will take each one of these possibilities in turn.

Employee beliefs and values

To be precise, organisations do not have goals. Only people have goals. Over the last 20 years there has been increasing emphasis on achieving change through aligning individual and corporate goals. If only there was congruence between corporate and individual goals, it is argued, most forms of management control would be rendered redundant.

People look for meaning in their work and to have their needs met. Abraham Maslow (1987) argues that we are motivated by the need to satisfy seven innate needs. See Figure 5.3.

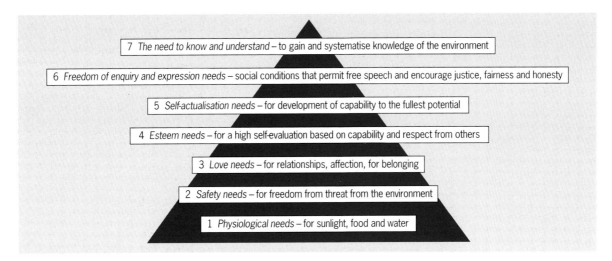

Figure 5.3 *Abraham Maslow's hierarchy of needs*

Source: *Adapted from Huczynski and Buchanan* (1991)

It is the higher-level needs that change managers can appeal to in designing change management programmes. Von Pierer at Siemens was clearly attempting to increase people's self-esteem and enable self-actualisation by devolving responsibility. At the same time, by creating a 'climate for honest open dialogue' and benchmarking against other industries, he was encouraging freedom of enquiry and understanding.

This approach does, however, have its dangers. 'People are our greatest asset' can soon become a meaningless slogan and cynicism sets in. Employees can quickly come to feel they are being manipulated unless they are genuinely empowered by the change programme. Finally, not all employees have, or need to have, the same value set.

Employee behaviour

Alternatively, we can set out to change employee behaviour. Here we are not addressing the employee's underlying value system, just asking them to behave in a different way.

For instance, management may believe that many of the delays in processing customer orders stem from a lack of co-operation between departments. The change management programme may set up new processes that require the individual to consult with other departments as an order is processed. The hope is that if this is seen to be a success, then the barriers between the different departments may come down as individuals identify more strongly with the whole company.

The argument is that the individual can only change if the organisational system in which they operate is changed. This focus on work-based behaviours can then be used to affect the individual's behaviour and perhaps ultimately their value systems.

Employee outputs

Finally, instead of attempting to change values or behaviour, should we simply concentrate instead on the outputs that employees produce? If, in the previous example, we set up targets for quality and meeting delivery deadlines in the processing of sales orders, we can perhaps leave it to the individuals concerned to sort out how best to meet the new targets.

The fundamental question is to what extent you provide a framework for groups of employees in terms of processes and procedures, and to what extent you tell them what you want and let them get on with it. The decision will vary according to the nature of the organisation and the type of person it employs. Where individuals seek a high degree of autonomy, such as medical staff or sales staff who are paid on commission, then this may be an important element in the change programme.

There were three key stakeholder groups at Secure Components whose specific needs had to be understood and sensitively addressed.

The first was the senior management group. Neil agreed that the operations director should take the role of programme champion. The terms of reference for this role included board lobbying, managing political issues, removing barriers to change, providing high-level leadership and generally working to protect the change programme. This also had the advantage of intimately involving the operations director, ensuring his active participation and continual support throughout.

The second was the middle management group. Arguably, they had the most to lose and the least to gain. Neil knew from previous experience that they could easily destabilise the change programme through coercive/directive management. To deal with this potential problem Neil took a proactive approach. He decided to involve key members of the middle management team in the change programme steering team. They would monitor progress and remove local barriers. Their participation would generate buy-in, provide the feeling of being in control and, importantly, control their desire to micro-manage. Neil largely sold their involvement on the basis of their personal development. For some, organisational changes may lead to redundancy. Their involvement, and support, was encouraged on the basis of personal development and the prospect of involvement in future change projects.

Neil also recognised that he had to be very sensitive to the middle management performance drivers.

Reward systems based on meeting budgeted internal performance measures may be compromised by the change process, or worse still, compromised by the future state. An analysis of the reward system revealed the need to negotiate lower performance targets to ensure appropriate behaviours during the transition phase. New performance measures and targets would be needed in the future.

The third group was the workforce. Neil found this group very suppressed and, he believed, very under-utilised. The purpose of the programme was to empower them to shape their own environment. Workshops and training sessions were designed to give them the skills and confidence to participate and contribute to the change programme effectively.

Ask yourself:

◆ *Neil had carefully laid the groundwork, but what could still go wrong during future stages of the change management programme?*

Activity 14
Individual change objectives

Objectives

Use this activity to:

◆ evaluate different approaches for different target groups within an organisation

◆ determine whether you are trying to change people's values, behaviours or outputs.

Case study

Read through the following case study.

Change at Ericsson Australia

In the early 1990s, the MD of Ericsson Australia, Kjell Sorme, attempted to change the organisation from a bureaucratic, technology-focused company, to one with a focus on customer service as well as engineering. Specialist customer divisions became the drivers of the business, with the more technical divisions, such as design and engineering, supporting them. The workforce was reduced from 2,500 to 1,800, with the largest cuts in manufacturing. New recruits have been taken on since, but into service and marketing roles.

By 1993, despite additional initiatives such as a mission statement, a strategic plan and many change projects, it was realised that these initiatives alone were insufficient. They did not enable individuals to understand in what way they had to change. Therefore, a new mission statement was developed for Ericsson, and a programme called Leading Change put in place for all senior and middle managers, which ran from October 1993 to March 1994.

The main focus of Leading Change was to challenge the existing way of thinking within the organisation, and to better equip managers with the necessary change skills. Each programme started with an address on the need for change from Sorme, followed by video interviews with Ericsson customers. These interviews contained the customers' assessment of their relationship with Ericsson and their future expectations. The rest of the course introduced the managers to a number of change tools tailored to suit Ericsson's needs. The aim of these tools was not only to challenge existing mindsets, but also to encourage the programme participants to have a commitment to the changes needed at Ericsson as well as a sense of urgency.

Source: *Adapted from Graetz (1996), quoted in Balogun and Hailey (1999)*

Task

Compare the experiences of Ericsson here with those of Siemens set out on page 101. In what ways was the organisation attempting to change values, behaviour and outputs?

	Ericsson	Siemens
Values		
Behaviour		
Outputs		

Feedback

Set out below are some examples for each of the headings. You may have drawn further ones from the case study.

	Ericsson	*Siemens*
Values	Leading change programme challenged existing thinking and gained commitment for change	Whole programme sought to challenge deeply held beliefs
Behaviour	Leading change programme designed to provide new skills, which enable new forms of behaviour	Employees paid by results Stock-option plans introduced
Outputs	The initial reorganisation into specialist customer divisions will have been primarily aimed at outputs. This was shown to be insufficient	ToP aimed to improve growth, profitability and innovation Benchmark studies

Organisational dynamics

At the start of the change management programme you will need to establish a partnership between the change management team and the rest of the workforce. As time passes and everyone gets further into the change programme, so the nature of the partnership will change. A process of organisational learning will be taking place.

The evolutionary model

The evolutionary model set out in Figure 5.4 is adapted from Doz (1996) and considers what differentiates a successful development of the change programme from the unsuccessful.

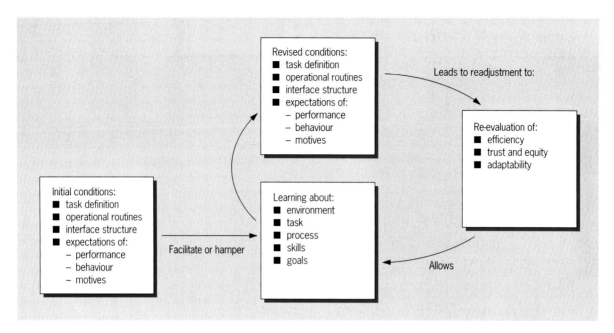

Figure 5.4 *Simplified process of project evolution*

Source: *Adapted from Doz* (1996)

The initial conditions on the left of the figure comprise:

♦ definition of the objectives and scope of the change management project teams

♦ the procedures, or quality systems, to be used during the programme

♦ how the different groups involved in the change management programme will interface

♦ the expectations people have about the performance, behaviour and motives of the change management team.

How these initial conditions are put in place will either facilitate or hamper the project teams' and other stakeholders' learning about:

♦ the organisation and environment that they are seeking to change

♦ how to work together to achieve change

♦ the respective skills of the different team members

♦ each other's goals and objectives.

Stakeholders in the change programme will continually monitor the programme and each other and re-evaluate:

- ◆ the efficiency with which the early changes are being implemented
- ◆ whether the contribution to, and the effect upon, all the different stakeholders is equitably distributed
- ◆ whether people are genuinely adapting to the changes being made or whether the effects will be only temporary.

This re-evaluation will inform the decision making in the programme and establish revised conditions. These revised conditions may be anything from a fine-tune of the initial conditions to a complete rethink of the programme's objectives or how the change process operates.

The message of this model is an important one. You must be willing, if contributing to a wide-ranging change management programme, to see your initial assessment and objectives rewritten as the programme evolves over time. Successful change programmes evolve through a sequence of learning, re-evaluation and readjustment cycles, in which the influence of the initial conditions quickly fades away.

Conversely, sticking blindly to the initial plan of action can be disastrous. Unsuccessful change programme organisations are characterised by poor learning, or total absence of learning, where initial conditions are maintained and the change programme fails.

Look carefully at Table 5.3, which sets out characteristics of static and evolutionary change. The initial conditions of the change programme either facilitate or hamper the learning process and lead to positive or negative evolution respectively.

	Static	Evolutionary
Task definition	Rigidly defined tasks Narrow skill base Top management lead	Generic definition with defined boundaries Complementary and overlapping skill base Autonomous team championing
Organisational routines	Strong functional alignment Organisational fragmentation Major pace differences Embedded routines, defensive behaviour	Cross-functional emphasis Integrated and quality communication Similar pace of decision making Desire for joint development of more effective routines
Interface structure	Formal or unstructured interfaces Inconsistent and contrary management decision making Changes in key personnel	Readiness to allow interfaces to evolve Reinforcement of importance of change through management decision making and wider communications Continuity of key personnel
Expectations	Initial optimistic/ambitious expectations Conflicting terms of reference Individual-based benefits Ambiguity and poor information	Realistic and flexible expectations Similar/compatible terms of reference Value creation and team-based benefits Limited ambiguity and access to timely, relevant information

Table 5.3 *Characteristics of static and evolutionary change*

Source: *Adapted from Doz (1996)*

For a successful and sustainable change programme, it is important to develop the features in the evolutionary column. Where your change programme shows the static characteristics, then failure is a real possibility. Positive re-evaluation creates a virtuous circle where increased stakeholder confidence leads to positive evolutionary organisational learning and development.

How can change be enjoyed rather than endured?

The best change management programmes are periods when individuals feel a great sense of creative energy. Possibly for the first time, they have been asked to contribute ideas and to become involved. Working together as a member of the team drawn from a number of departments can also provide its own new, invigorating experience.

Table 5.4 sets out the questions you need to consider in order to set up a change programme where everyone will enjoy, rather than endure, the experience.

What personal benefit will be gained by individuals involved?	Active participation in the change process depends on the extent to which the needs, attitudes and beliefs of individual employees are taken into account
What is the view of the official/unofficial leader(s) of the workgroups involved?	The expectations and opinions of those in prestige positions tend to carry more weight than the members of their workgroups and/or the influence of the staff 'trainer'
What fresh, objective information is available about the need for change?	Data centred on one's own organisation or group is more meaningful and influential than more generalised information about attitudes and behaviour
To what extent are facts pertinent to the change process generated from within the workgroup?	The planning, gathering, analysis and interpretation of diagnostic data by the individuals and groups involved are more likely to be understood and accepted than those presented by outside experts
To what degree can those involved in the change influence the change process?	Complete participation by all the members of the affected workgroups is likely to be most effective. However, participation by representatives of the group and/or the supervisor only can reduce the amount of overt opposition
How attractive is the workgroup to its members?	When change is being proposed, group cohesiveness (which will be high if the group satisfies the needs of its members) will operate to reduce resistance to change if the group sees the changes as beneficial. This is because strong group membership tends to lead to greater individual conformity to group norms
Does the change process involve taking individuals away from their job into temporary groups, or does it involve individuals in their usual workgroup setting?	Change programmes that involve individuals within the context of their immediate job situation are likely to be more successful because this group has more psychological meaning to an individual than does a group with only temporary membership
How open are the communication channels relating to the need for, plans for and consequence of change?	Change processes that provide specific knowledge on the progress to date, and specify the criteria against which improvement is to be measured, are most successful in establishing and maintaining change

Table 5.4 *How can change be enjoyed rather than endured?*
Source: *Adapted from Huse* (1980) *by Mabey et al.* (1998)

This summary picks up several themes, which have been discussed throughout this book. When you contribute to a change management programme, do not concentrate on recommending the right answers. Instead, look at your fellow workers and seek their ideas and contributions.

This is much more difficult than a top-down approach to management, but also much more fun. Where empowerment of the workforce becomes a reality rather than a slogan, real competitive advantages in terms of the creativity, efficiency and effectiveness of your organisation are sure to follow.

Secure Components had undergone a radical transformation. It had suffered for years with its 'traditional' cultural roots, and in the space of 12 months had reinvented itself. It had learnt a precious commodity, the process of evolutionary change.

Key to this transformation was the tailored change management framework comprising credible operational and cultural vision, a clear (situationally led) environmental perspective and a stakeholder population who were prepared to listen and act.

Successful change programmes also require effective change leaders. People, who can see the bigger picture, sell their ideas, care for people, motivate others and themselves, have the courage to challenge the status quo, use initiative to break through barriers, tolerance of uncertainty and, above all, have a great sense of humour.

Secure Components had learnt to work smarter. It had reinvented a traditional mode of organisation and operation. The corporate director of the group was so impressed with the transformation he declared 'the Secure Components' way' the new corporate operations model to which all group companies should aspire. Customer feedback was equally commendatory.

Reject rates were down 40 per cent, productivity was up 50 per cent, on-time delivery was up 50 per cent, cycle times were down 80 per cent, the need for temporary staff was eliminated, employee morale had never been higher and absenteeism had plummeted.

You might comment: 'This was all good news for Secure Components but my organisation's problems are unique and our industry has special needs. The business continuity risk of this type of change programme vastly outweighs the potential benefits.' Before the change programme, Secure Components had said the very same things and had the very same concerns. These were concerns that were based on failed change initiatives from the past and represent the initial conditions that quickly faded during their evolutionary learning change programme.

This case study, the change process, the people and business performance improvements achieved should not be an isolated example. There is no reason why your organisation should not, and cannot, achieve an equally impressive transformation.

Ask yourself:

- *Why can your organisation not achieve similar improvements?*
- *What attributes of yourself do you see in the description of a successful change leader?*

Activity 15
Sustainable change

Objectives

This activity will help you to:

- explore the importance of organisational dynamics in the change process
- evaluate how to sustain a culture of change for the future.

Case study

Read through this final case study on the experiences of Secure Components.

Organisational dynamics

Neil considered initiating a series of evolutionary learning cycles to be the Holy Grail of change management. This was the only true source of sustainable competitive advantage.

The operational vision that Neil had launched was: 'We will learn to work smarter to create a lean operation that focuses on exceeding customer expectations and establishes us as the best in the business'.

But the operational vision needed to be underpinned with a cultural vision. The cultural vision was based upon four key dimensions: customer focus, cross-functional teamworking and communications, empowerment and responsibility, and making money.

Together, the operational vision and the cultural vision established the standards against which the participant stakeholders would judge the legitimacy of future actions, decisions and the success of the change programme.

Following on directly from the workplace reorganisation, Neil launched two key initiatives designed to catalyse organisational learning. The first was a managed programme of continuous improvement, and the second was a structured and targeted business process improvement methodology.

The continuous improvement programme (CIP) comprised an organisation of cross-functional teams each working on their own project.

Similarly, the business process improvement programme (BPI) comprised cross-functional teams but this time working on specific segments of a targeted business process. Each team would make improvements that contributed to a joint objective.

In both cases, each project team had formal terms of reference, a facilitator, a leader and stretch goals. Each team reported progress to their peer groups and the management steering team, but fundamentally had full autonomy. The facilitator was responsible for ensuring that the team had the necessary resources, supporting training and that it kept aligned with the operational and cultural vision.

The role of the facilitator was key to the sustainability of these programmes. Carefully selected and trained, the facilitators were the resources that would develop and manage the change flux, initially in the reorganised workplace arena, and ultimately throughout the rest of the organisation.

Through a series of positive re-evaluation–readjustment cycles, Neil watched the organisation learn the process of evolutionary change. Very quickly, the initial reactions ('It won't last, it's just another management fad') faded and the organisation began to learn how to improve and how to exceed customer expectations. This is the source of sustained competitive advantage.

Task

Evaluate the Secure Components change programme using the structure provided by the 'simplified process of project evolution' set out in Figure 5.4 and illustrated again here.

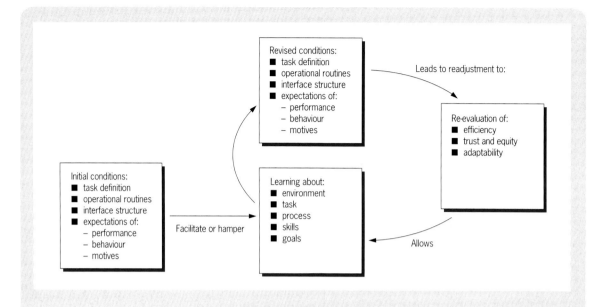

Separately identify:

◆ the initial conditions

◆ the learning stage

◆ revised conditions

◆ re-evaluation

Feedback

The initial conditions were of mistrust and cynicism about the possibility for change. The project was organised in such a way that there was clarity of purpose and involvement by the whole workforce.

From the outset of the project the different teams learnt more about the organisation they were seeking to change, but also about what their colleagues had to contribute and the possibilities of change. Through training programmes and constant interaction in the workplace, new skills were acquired.

The changing management style from directive to collaborative signalled evidence of equity and adaptability in its dealings with the workforce. The CIP and BPI programmes illustrated the organisation's commitment to efficiency and adaptability. As the benefits became evident, participants re-evaluated the programme and their contribution.

This led to establishing revised conditions, not just once or twice during the course of the project, but as an ongoing part of the new culture of the organisation. This ability to constantly renew the way of 'doing things around here' provides the basis for sustainable competitive advantage.

◆ Recap

In this theme we explore the means to sustain change and manage organisational dynamics.

Identify possible launch strategies

◆ A successful launch shows that change is possible, builds momentum for the transition period and shows the possibilities of a better tomorrow.

◆ The way in which a change project is defined affects its acceptability to those who are going to be affected.

Consider how different styles of managing change may be appropriate in different contexts

◆ Broadly, the choice of management style lies on the continuum from coercion to democracy.

◆ Your choice of style will be influenced by such factors as the urgency of the change, the nature of the workforce and the nature of the organisation's products.

Evaluate different approaches for different target groups within an organisation

◆ The individuals that make up an organisation are not a homogeneous body. Different groups within the organisation will have their own priorities and agendas.

♦ You need to decide what it is you are trying to change: is it the values held, the way people behave or simply the expected outputs?

Explore the importance of organisational dynamics in the change process and how to sustain a culture of change for the future

♦ Doz (1996) sets out a virtuous circle of implementation, where the initial conditions give rise to organisational learning, which causes people to reassess those initial conditions.

♦ This then gives rise to revised conditions, which themselves provide opportunities for further organisational learning.

 More @

Campbell, D., Stonehouse, G. and Houston, B. (2002) 2nd edition, *Business Strategy: an Introduction*, Elsevier Butterworth-Heinemann
This is an accessible textbook that provides a straightforward and comprehensive guide to complex issues and concepts. See Chapter 10 for the strategic implementation of change.

Dixon, R. (2003) 3rd edition, *The Management Task*, Elsevier Butterworth-Heinemann
This book considers the nature of management and the environment in which management operates. The requirements for effective, successful management techniques are explored, covering leadership in Part 2, Chapter 6. It presents a concise overview of a wide range of leadership models.

Kanter, R. M. (1992) *The Change Masters: Corporate Entrepreneurs at Work*, International Thomson Business Press
This is a classic and well-respected text on change management and the impact of change programmes at work.

Mullins, L. J. (1999) 5th edition, *Management and Organisational Behaviour*, Financial Times Pitman Publishing
Taking a managerial approach and demonstrating the application of behavioural science within the workplace, this text emphasises the role of management as a core integrating activity. Look here for a useful summary of the approaches taken by different writers on management styles.

Thomson, R. (2002) 3rd edition, *Managing People*, Elsevier Butterworth-Heinemann
Managing People addresses the perspective of the individual manager whose role includes the management of people, as well as issues

concerning the organisation as a whole. See particularly Chapter 11 'Managing in a changing world'.

The Change Management Resource Library –
www.change-management.org/articles.htm
This website offers a wide range of useful and interesting articles on the subject of change management. For instance:

◆ 'Building Successful Teams in the Midst of Transition', by Thomas W. McKee
Some people seem to thrive on change. How do they do it? How do they manage change in a way that they not only survive, but also excel?

◆ 'Change Leaders: The New Commandments of Change', by Peter F. Drucker
Here's all that's certain about the future: it holds profound and unpredictable change. But as smart CEOs have already learned, that's all you need to know to prepare your organisation.

◆ 'Change Management Roles of Executive Sponsors', by Project Phase
Senior managers play a critical role in change management, and that role changes depending on the stage of the change initiative.

References

Allen, L. (1973) *Professional Management*, McGraw-Hill

Argyris, C. (1977) 'Double loop learning in organisations', *Harvard Business Review,* Sept-Oct , 115–25

Black, J. S. (2001) 'Time to get back to the basics', in Mastering People Management section of *Finanical Times* 19 November

Balogun, J. and Hailey, V. (1999) *Exploring Strategic Change*, Financial Times Prentice Hall

Burnes, B. (1996*) Managing Change: A Strategic Approach to Organisational Dynamics*, Pitman Publishing

Carnall, C. (1999) 2nd edition, *Managing Change in Organisations,* Financial Times Prentice Hall

Doz, Y. L. (1996) 'The Evolution of Co-operation in Strategic Alliances: Initial Conditions or Learning Processes?' *Strategic Management Journal*, Vol. 17

Eglin, R. (2001), 'Inspired leaders can revamp a company', *Sunday Times*, 8 July source Credit Suisse First Boston

Fayol, H. (1949) *General and Industrial Management*, Pitman Publishing

Goodstein, L. D. and Burke, W. W. (1991) 'Creating Successful Organisational Change', *Organisational Dynamics,* Vol. 19/4, 5–17

Grundy, A. (1995) *Breakthrough Strategies for Growth*, Financial Times Prentice Hall

Haberberg, A. and Rieple, A. (2001) *The Strategic Management of Organisations*, Financial Times, Prentice Hall

Huczynski, A. and Buchanan, D. (1991) *Organizational Change,* Financial Times Prentice Hall

Huse, E. F. (1980) 2nd edition, *Organization development and change,* West Publishing Co.

Johnson, G. and Scholes, K. (1999) 2nd edition, *Exploring Corporate Strategy*, Prentice Hall Europe

Kanter, R. M. (1983) *The Change Masters: Corporate Entrepreneurs at Work*, George Allen & Unwin

Katzenbach, J. R. (1996) 'Real Change Leaders: How you Can Create Growth and High Performance at your Company', *McKinsey Quarterly,* Nicholas Brealey Publishing, *No. 1, 148–163*

Lewin, K. (1952) *Field Theory in Social Science*, Harper and Row

Lynch, R. (2000) *Corporate Strategy*, Financial Times Prentice Hall

Mabey, C., Salaman, G. and Storey, J. (1998) *Human Resource Management: A Strategic Introduction*, Blackwell Business

Management Today (1996) 'Asda's Open Plan', December

Maslow, A. H. (1987) 3rd edition, *Motivation and Personality*, Harper and Row

Mintzberg, H. (1973) *The Nature of Managerial Work*, Prentice Hall

Mullins, L. J. (1999) 5th edition, *Management and Organisational Behaviour*, Financial Times Prentice Hall

Pacanowsky, M. E. and O'Donnell-Trujillo, N. (1982) 'Communication and organizational culture', *The Western Journal of Speech Communications*, Vol. 46, Spring, 115-30

Paton, R. and McCalman, J. (2000) 2nd edition, *Change Management: a Guide to Effective Implementation*, SAGE Publications

Robbins, S. P. (1993) *Organizational Behaviour*, Prentice Hall International

Sadler, P. (1995) *Managing Change*, Kogan Page

Schein, E. H. (1992) *Organizational Culture and Leadership*, Jossey-Bass

Schein, E. (1993) 'On dialogue, culture and organizational learning', *Organizational Dynamics*, Autumn, 44–51

Schön, D. A. and Argyris, C. (1996) *Organisational Learning II*, Addison-Wesley

Senge, P. (1992) *The Fifth Discipline: The art and practice of the learning organization*, Doubleday

Senior, B. (1997) *Organisational Change*, Pitman Publishing

Stacey, R. D. (1996) *Strategic Management and Organisation Dynamics*, Pitman Publishing

Strebel, P. (1997) 'Breakpoint: how to stay in the game', *Mastering Management*, Part 17, Financial Times Pitman Publishing

Strebel, P. (1997) 'Choosing the right change path', *Mastering Management*, Part 17, Financial Times Pitman Publishing

Wolf, M. (2001) 'hp ads celebrate inventors', www.hp.com/hpinfo/newsroom/feature_stories/hpads2001.htm